STEP-BY-STEP CRAFTS

Pergamano®
PARCHMENT
CRAFT

STEP-BY-STEP CRAFTS

Pergamano® PARCHMENT CRAFT

MARTHA OSPINA

CREATIVE
PUBLISHING
international

MINNETONKA, MINNESOTA

First published in 2002 in the USA and Canada by
Creative Publishing international, Inc.

5900 Green Oak Drive
Minnetonka, MN 55343
1-800-328-3895

Published in the United Kingdom by New Holland
Publishers (UK) Ltd

ISBN 1-58923-020-5

Photographer: John Freeman
Editor: Clare Hubbard
Assistant Editor: Emily Preece-Morrison
Production: Hazel Kirkman
Editorial Direction: Rosemary Wilkinson

10 9 8 7 6 5 4 3 2 1

Reproduction by PICA Colour Separation, Singapore
Printed and bound in Malaysia by Times Offset
(M) Sdn. Bhd.

Library of Congress Cataloging-in-Publication Data

Ospina, Martha.
    Parchment craft / Martha Ospina.
      p. cm. -- (Step-by-step crafts)
    Includes index.
    ISBN 1-58923-020-5 (pbk.)
    1. Paper work. 2. Parchment. I. Title. II. Series.
TT870 .08697 2002
745.54--dc21
                                2001047053

Acknowledgements

Many thanks to: Peter Venema of Pergamano
International for supplying the Pergamano
materials that I have used extensively in this
book; my husband Tiemen for his support;
Linda, Mieke, Wilma and the other
Pergamano teachers who all lent a hand to
help me finish the artwork in time.

Contents

Introduction

Today the material used in parchment craft is a heavy type of parchment paper that is similar to the original parchment used thousands of years ago. It is strong, translucent, suitable to paint on and easy to perforate, cut and fold. Parchment was invented in the Turkish city of Bergama (Pergamum in Latin) when people had to find an alternative to papyrus due to the local wars that were preventing the importation of its raw materials. Throughout history parchment has been used for many different purposes – books, important documents, paintings and wall decorations. Parchment art was exclusively European until early in the sixteenth century when European settlers took the craft to South America, where it became extremely popular and remains so today.

In Colombia, my native country, people like to send handmade parchment invitations and greeting cards. When I was 14 years old I made many of these cards for *Quinceañeras*, girls celebrating their 15th birthday. At this age girls are considered to be adults and a party is held to mark the occasion. The cards were very popular and it was through making them that I became skilled in parchment craft and earned some pocket money.

After moving to the Netherlands in 1986 I continued to practice parchment craft, creating designs for books and developing new materials. Even after all these years, my pleasure in the craft remains undiminished. It is a creative activity, offering an almost unlimited range of possibilities. A little bit of my heart goes into every project I make.

Upon moving to Holland, it was parchment craft that helped me to learn the Dutch language, to become accustomed to my new home and to make new friends.

I hear similar stories from other enthusiasts at craft fairs and exhibitions. Having this kind of feedback brings me great happiness and encourages me to continue my work. I feel very privileged to do this interesting work and to have my hobby as my profession.

I am grateful to the publishers for the opportunity to produce a second book about this craft. The easiest way to learn about parchment craft is through step-by-step instructions accompanied by clear, informative photographs and this is exactly what this book offers. Thorough instruction in the basic techniques is included for the beginner as well as more elaborate, inspirational projects for those with some experience.

For those of you who wish to learn more and attend a parchment craft course, details of the worldwide qualified teacher network are provided on page 96. It has been established by the International Parchment Craft Academy, of which I am the president.

I am sure this book will be a great source of information and inspiration to you and I hope it will give you many hours of pleasure.

With love

Martha Ospina

Getting Started

Start by carefully reading the sections on materials and basic techniques. This way you will get an overall idea about parchment craft and how it is created. Beginners should first of all do the exercises on pages 11 to 19. Even those who are more experienced may find it interesting to do the exercises and compare their results with the pictures.

The exercises detail the basic techniques of parchment craft. Repeat them until you are satisfied with the results you achieve. Once you can cut ten crosses well, you will be able to move on and work a large project neatly. The projects develop from simple items to more elaborate designs. I suggest working through them in book order, particularly if you are a beginner.

The materials needed for each project are listed. You should always have Perga-Soft, paper towels, an old cloth and a bowl of water on hand. The templates and the working descriptions are all based on Pergamano materials, the code numbers of which are listed in the text. By using these materials you will find it easy to follow the step-by-step instructions that accompany each project and you will be confident that your perforating tools will match the perforating grids on the templates.

A number of parchment creations based on the templates in the book are shown in the galleries. Sometimes only a part of a template is used, part of it may have been enlarged or another design or parts of designs are used. As you gain in confidence, you will be able to create designs based on the templates in this book.

MATERIALS

Below is a list of the Pergamano materials used in this book (see page 96 for suppliers). For inks and paints, the complete color ranges are given although not all the colors have been used in the projects in this book.

Parchment papers
Pergamano parchment (1481): standard, grey-colored, 150 gsm/m², size 11" x 8" (297 x 210 mm), 25 sheets in a pack. Parchment of 150 gsm is suitable for most projects, but for larger projects or applications where a stronger parchment is required, parchment with a weight of 175 gsm can be used. This is available in a pack of 12 sheets, A3 size (1403).

Pergamano Rainbow parchment (1483): five different color patterns, 150 gsm/m², size 11" x 8" (297 x 210 mm), 10 sheets in a pack. This parchment is rainbow-colored, with the color beams arranged both horizontally and vertically across the sheets. Because the color is only on one side of the parchment, embossing will produce a highlighted effect on the colored side and a white effect on the reverse side of the sheet. Pergamano Rainbow Pastel parchment (1484) is also available, 10 sheets in a pack.

Pergamano Fantasy parchment I (1476): five strong colors – red, turquoise, yellow, blue and white, 200 gsm/m², size 9" x 13" (250 x 350 mm), 10 sheets in a pack.

Pergamano Fantasy parchment II (1477): five soft colors – lilac, brown, ochre, ivory and light green, 160 gsm/m², size 9" x 13" (250 x 350 mm), 10 sheets in a pack. Fantasy parchment is colored on both sides.

Other Pergamano parchment papers, e.g. marbled, are also available but these are not used in this book. For more information on these products, contact your local supplier.

Embossing tools and pad

Ball shaped embossing tools: large ball (1102), small ball (1101), extra small ball (1107). These tools are used to emboss areas of parchment design.

Fine stylus embossing tool (1103): for embossing fine lines.

HockeyStick (1100): this tool enables you to create shadowing effects.

Star-Tool (1122): used to emboss decorative stars.

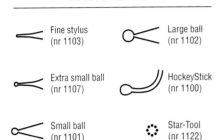

EMBOSSING TOOLS

Fine stylus (nr 1103)		Large ball (nr 1102)	
Extra small ball (nr 1107)		HockeyStick (nr 1100)	
Small ball (nr 1101)		Star-Tool (nr 1122)	

Perga-Soft: a spot of this product on the embossing tool makes embossing easier.

"De Luxe" embossing pad (1413): this pad must be used when embossing parchment. The top is soft, therefore the parts of the parchment that are embossed become raised.

Perforating tools and pad

Thin-handle perforating tools: 1-needle tool (1104), 2-needle tool (1106), 3-needle tool (1108), 4-needle tool (1105), 5-needle tool (1112), 7-needle (also called "Flower-Tool") tool (1111).

Thick-handle perforating tools: Straight-Four (1118), Semi-Square (1114), Semi-Star (1117), Semi-Circle (1109), Four-in-Four (1113) and Heart-Shape (1116). The needles are positioned in a wider pattern than those described above.

"Excellent" perforating pad (1419): this soft pad should be placed underneath the parchment while perforating.

PERFORATING TOOLS

1-needle (nr 1104)		Flower Tool (nr 1111)	
2-needle (nr 1106)		Semi-Circle (nr 1109)	
3-needle (nr 1108)		Four-in-Four (nr 1113)	
4-needle (nr 1105)		Semi-Square (nr 1114)	
5-needle (nr 1112)		Semi-Star (nr 1117)	
Straight-Four (nr 1118)		Heart-Shape (nr 1116)	

Perforating grids and tools

As well as perforating parchment by using a template with a dotted grid, you can practice a different perforating technique using a metal grid. Two grids with metal gauze are available, which act as a guide to full perforating or perforating into a pattern by counting.

Easy-Grid Regular Mesh (1460): the "Excellent" perforating pad fits exactly underneath the frame. The pad gives contrast and support to the gauze. The regular mesh has 18 square holes per 1" (2 cm).

Easy-Grid Fine Mesh (1461): this grid is similar to the regular one but the mesh has 25 holes per 1" (2 cm).

"Diamond" perforating tool (1121): this tool can be used on both types of Easy-Grid. It has a conical square point that only penetrates 2 mm into the grid if no force is applied, making tiny square holes in the parchment.

"Arrow" perforating tool (1124): this tool fulfils the same function as the "Diamond" tool but it has a conical round point and makes tiny round holes in the parchment.

Coloring products

Tinta inks are waterproof, water-based inks used for tracing templates onto parchment or for painting with. They are one of the easier products with which to apply color and give a transparent matte result. Bear in mind when undertaking a project, that they do take some time to dry. The colors are: white 01T, blue 02T, red 03T, green 04T, turquoise 05T, orange 06T, violet 07T, leaf green 10T, black 11T, sepia 12T, yellow 16T, fuchsia 20T, silver 21T, gold 22T.

Tinta-Pearl inks give a pearlized finish. The colors are: white 1TP, blue 2TP, red 3TP, sepia 12TP, yellow 16TP.

Pintura paints are acrylic-based and dry quicker than Tinta inks. They give good coverage on parchment and produce a slightly glossy finish. The colors are: white 01, blue 02, red 03, light green 04, ochre 05, orange 06, violet 07, green 08, black 11, brown 12, skin color 13, yellow 16, fuchsia 20, grey 34, turquoise 48, bordeaux 51, cinnamon 52.

Pinta-Perla paints are similar to the Pintura paints but produce a pearlized effect on the parchment. The colors are: white 01N, blue 02N, red 03N, light green 04N, violet 07N, green 08N, brown 12N, skin color 13N, yellow 16N, fuchsia 20N, bronze 30N.

Using Perga-Color Exclusive felt-tip pens (1431) is perhaps the easiest way to begin painting on parchment. The felt-tips are used straight onto the parchment or can be applied with a brush for shadowing (light-dark effects). Box 1431 contains 20 numbered colors.

Dorso crayons make it easy to color standard white parchment. The color is applied on the reverse side of the parchment and then spread evenly over the desired area. There are two different boxed sets, each containing eight different colors: Dorso Box 1 (1440): violet, magenta, blue, yellow-ochre, skin, yellow, light green, turquoise; Dorso Box 2 (1442): light blue, red, brown, orange, lilac, green, light brown, black.

Miscellaneous

Mapping pen with nib (1420): used with Tinta inks to trace templates onto parchment. The nib can be inserted into the handle to protect it from damage.

Paintbrush size 2, sable (1422): the hairs are organic and should be handled with care. Point the bristles after use.

Paintbrush size 0, sable (1421): this is used to paint tiny details.

Paintbrush size 2, Kolinsky (1425): the best brush for painting on parchment.

Perga-Color brush size 6 (1426): a stiff-haired brush used with Perga-Color Exclusive felt-tip pens.

Pergamano sponge (1449): for keeping paintbrushes moist.

Pergamano scissors (1132): fine pointed scissors used mainly for cutting perforated areas into crosses and slits.

Pinking shears: cut decorative edges.

Transparent, non-permanent tape: useful as it can easily be removed.

Pergakit glue (1411): used for 3D work.

White pencil (9202): for tracing folds.

BEFORE YOU START

For this craft you need a steady table, a comfortable straight-backed chair and, most important, a good source of light shining directly onto your work. Protect your table against damage from sharp tools and ink spillages. It is important to keep the parchment clean while working. Wash your hands before you start and protect your work by having some paper towel or tissue underneath your hand.

BASIC TECHNIQUES

In the following exercises, the terms BT1, BT2, etc. refer to the templates on page 84.

Tracing a template

You will need
Parchment paper, standard
Template BT1 (page 84)
Adhesive tape, non-permanent
Tinta ink: white 01T
Mapping pen
Cloth or tissue
Bowl of water
Tinta ink: gold 22T
Wooden stick

1 Place a piece of parchment 5" x 4" (147 x 105 mm) over the template and stick it down with two pieces of adhesive tape, rolled up with the adhesive side outside. Press the parchment paper down to flatten the tape.

2 Shake the bottle of Tinta white ink well and unscrew the lid. Pull the nib out of the mapping pen, turn it and re-insert it into the pen the opposite way out.

3 Dip the mapping pen into the ink until the little hole in the nib is filled. Tap off excess ink on the rim of the bottle to avoid the risk of blots.

4 Draw some lines on a scrap piece of parchment, holding the pen at an angle. Do not press too hard or the points of the nib will open preventing the ink from flowing. New nibs can be greasy; if necessary, clean repeatedly with water and a cloth. Once you have got used to the feel of the pen, trace the entire design. Try to draw fine lines; the finer the lines, the nicer the result will be.

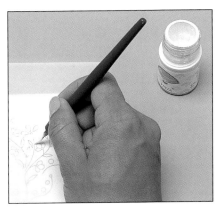

Tracing with gold ink

1 Trace template BT1 once more with Tinta gold ink. Because gold ink contains particles that settle at the bottom of the bottle, you will need to stir it with a small stick each time before use. An alternative way of getting the ink onto the nib is to dip your stirring stick into the bottom of the bottle and transfer the ink from it onto the nib.

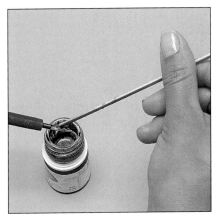

2 Trace the entire design with the gold ink.

Embossing

Embossing is to raise parts of the design by rubbing the parchment on the reverse side with ball-shaped tools.

You will need
Template BT1 (page 84)
Parchment paper, standard
Mapping pen
Tinta ink: white 01T
"De Luxe" embossing pad
Perga-Soft
Large ball embossing tool
Small ball embossing tool
Extra small ball embossing tool
Fine stylus embossing tool
HockeyStick embossing tool

Trace the design using the mapping pen and white ink. Leave to dry. Place your traced design facedown on the embossing pad. Perga-Soft makes the movement of the metal ball on the parchment smoother and easier; lightly touch the surface of the Perga-Soft with the embossing tool.

Embossing a dot

Take the large ball embossing tool and emboss one of the larger dots. Apply light pressure initially and emboss the space slowly, using only up and down movements and working from left to right (1). Then repeat this movement from right to left, etc. (2). Increase the pressure on the tool as you work. When the space within the circle has become white, finish off by moving the tool in circles along the outline of the dot (3). The result should be an even and raised white dot. Always judge the result by looking at the front.

Emboss all circles and petals this way. Always use the largest embossing tool that fits the area. Small tools used on large areas tend to give an uneven result.

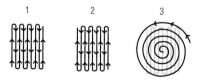

Grey tones

Lightly emboss the leaves to obtain a grey tone. Use the small ball tool for the large leaves and the extra small ball tool for the small leaves.

Embossing lines

Lines should be embossed with the fine stylus embossing tool. Emboss the single lines, holding the tool at an angle to avoid puncturing or scratching the parchment. Apply only gentle pressure; the smaller the tip of the tool, the lighter the pressure on it should be. (For very thin lines, the 1-needle perforating tool can be used.)

Shading

It is possible to obtain shading by embossing in tones ranging from light grey to white. This is done by selecting the appropriate embossing tool and by the intensity of the embossing.

You will need
Template BT2 (page 84)
Mapping pen
Tinta ink: white 01T
HockeyStick embossing tool (1100)

1 Trace the template using the mapping pen and the Tinta white ink. The curved bottom part of the HockeyStick tool is specially designed for embossing white tones gradually fading into grey. Try out the tool on a scrap piece of parchment, experimenting with the angle of the tool. Holding the HockeyStick in a vertical position will result in white; a more horizontal position will produce grey

4 Stippling is creating little white dots by hammering the parchment on the reverse side with the 1-needle tool. The needle makes tiny perforations. Before stippling always emboss the area lightly on the reverse side.

Leave the project facedown on the cardboard and remove the four pieces of adhesive tape. Take the 1-needle perforating tool and hammer the white areas in the picture. Start to stipple following the outline then work in horizontal lines moving downward. The needle's perforations should be close together and look even.

Obtain a whiter result by coloring the stippled area with a white pencil on the reverse side.

tones. Always hold the HockeyStick in such a way that its tip points towards the outline of the area you want to emboss. Study the picture of the embossed swan; try to obtain the same grey and white tones.

1 Trace template BT3 onto the parchment using a mapping pen and white ink. Leave to dry. Place the project facedown onto a piece of flat, hard cardboard. Stick the project onto the cardboard with a piece of adhesive tape on each of the four corners.

2 Select the blue crayon from Dorso Box 1 and gently apply some color in the center of the traced design. To avoid creating distinct lines do not press too hard as they may still show after spreading the color .

Dorsing and Stippling

With Dorso crayons you can color parchment with soft shades. The color is normally applied on the reverse side. At the front it will show as a soft and very even color tone.

You will need
Template BT3 (page 84)
Mapping pen
Tinta ink: white 01T
Parchment paper, standard
Hard, black flat cardboard
Adhesive tape, non-permanent
Dorso Box 1
Paper towel or soft cloth
Lavender oil or eucalyptus oil
Small ball embossing tool
1-needle perforating tool
White pencil

3 Apply a tiny dot of lavender or eucalyptus oil onto the cloth or paper towel and rub gently across the design to spread the color. Try to let the color fade out around the design.

5 Finish the project by embossing the remaining shapes of the project lightly along the outlines using the small ball embossing tool. Try to obtain the result shown in the picture.

Perforating with template underneath

You will need
Mapping pen
Template BT4 (page 84)
Tinta ink: white 01T
Parchment paper, standard
"De Luxe" embossing pad
Perga-Soft
Small ball embossing tool
"Excellent" perforating pad
Hard, flat cardboard
1- and 2-needle perforating tools
Straight-Four perforating tool
Ruler
Adhesive tape, non-permanent
4-needle perforating tool
5-needle perforating tool
Extra small embossing tool
Pergamano scissors
Craft knife

1 Using the mapping pen, trace the scalloped outlines of the template with Tinta white ink onto a piece of parchment. Remove the project from the template; place it facedown on the embossing pad and emboss between the scallops using the small ball embossing tool. Place the project faceup on the perforating pad. Put a piece of hard, flat cardboard underneath the pad to protect your table.

Perforate along the outside of the scallops using the 2-needle tool. To ensure an even distance between perforations, slide one needle into the last hole you have made. The tool will tend to lift the parchment; hold it in place with your fingers as you work.

For strong curved lines, it is better to use the 1-needle tool; for straight lines, you can also use the "Straight-Four" tool for a quicker result. For straight outlines you can perforate along the edge of a ruler.

2 Stick the project onto the template using two pieces of adhesive tape. Place the project faceup on the perforating pad. Take the 4-needle tool and perforate deep (there is no embossing) into the four-dot perforations of line 1. Hold the tool upright and position the needles precisely on the four dots. Perforate deep into the second line of perforations with the same tool. Then take the 5-needle tool and perforate the third line shallow. Then perforate the two bottom lines with the 4-needle tool (shallow). The needles of the tools will punch the parchment and the template together. In some projects there are often areas that should be embossed between the perforations. In this case you should first perforate shallow (approx. 1 mm), emboss this perforation and then perforate deep. This way the risk of damaging the parchment is reduced and the result will be more attractive.

3 Remove the template from the parchment and place the parchment facedown on the embossing pad. Using the extra small embossing tool, emboss the circles around the central holes of the 5-needle perforations (line 3), the small dot between the 4-needle perforations (line 4) and the ovals between the 4-needle perforations (line 5).

4 Place the parchment on the perforating pad. Now, twisting the tool gently, deeply perforate the shallow perforations.

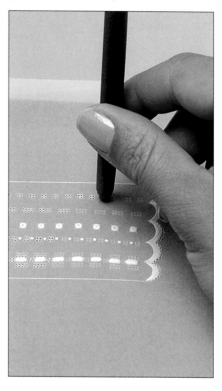

5 For cutting perforated borders and fine crosses use Pergamano scissors with fine-pointed blades. The following description is for right-handed people. With the points of the scissors pointing downwards, slide your index finger through the left scissor handle and support it with your thumb. Slide your third finger through the right scissor handle. The scissors open and close when you move the index finger and the third finger outwards and inwards. Getting used to handling these tiny scissors will take some practice.

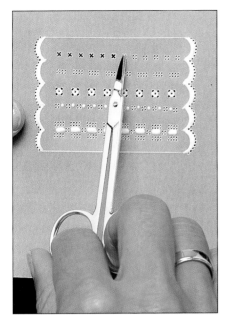
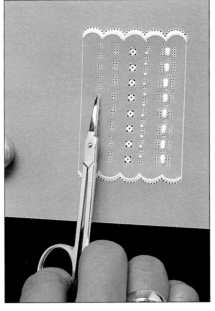
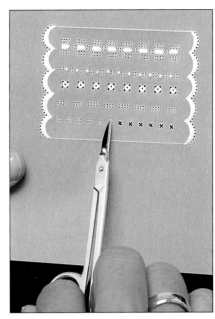

6 Hold the project in your left hand. Have the perforating pad underneath the parchment so you can see the perforations clearly. Insert the scissors into the upper two holes of one of the 4-needle perforations on line 1, taking care not to apply pressure. The position of the scissors should be almost flat in relation to the project, turn your wrist slightly to the left and cut (drawing 1).

7 Turn the project one-quarter counter-clockwise. Insert the blades of the scissors into the two top holes of the same 4-needle perforation and cut (drawing 2). Turn the project one-quarter turn counterclockwise and cut the upper two holes again (drawing 3). Turn the project a third time counterclockwise and cut the two upper holes (drawing 4). Now the tiny piece of parchment will fall out and the finished cross will be seen (drawing 5). The best way to cut out crosses is to cut all the upper holes of the row of 4-needle combinations first, then turn the project one-quarter and cut all the upper holes and so on, rather than cutting each individual cross one at a time.

8 If your cutting does not look as perfect as the examples in this picture, do not worry. Continue to experiment until you find the correct movement. It takes some time to become proficient in the unaccustomed sideways movement of your thumb and index finger. Using this technique cut the crosses of lines 1 and 4. Then, cut slits between the 4-needle perforations of rows 2 and 5. Slits are cut out as shown in drawing 6.

9 Cut the perforations along the outside of the two scalloped side borders. Open the scissors slightly so their points span the distance between two holes. Insert the points gently into two holes and cut the perforations along the scallops working from left to right. Finally, cut along the straight side borders with a craft knife to finish the project.

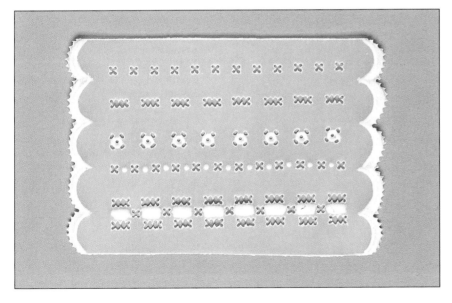

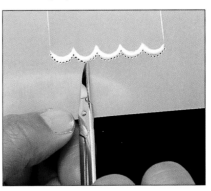

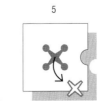
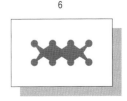

1   2   3   4   5   6

Perforating with Easy-Grid Regular Mesh

You will need
Easy-Grid Regular Mesh
"Excellent" perforating pad
Parchment paper, standard
Medical adhesive tape
"Diamond" perforating tool
Templates BT5-1 and BT5-2 (page 84)
Paintbrush no.2
Tinta ink: white 01T
Pergamano scissors

1 The Easy-Grid is a piece of metal gauze used as a guide when perforating straight horizontal lines, working from the top down, with no template underneath the parchment. Perforation patterns can be made by counting holes, as in cross-stitch embroidery. Place the "Excellent" perforating pad inside the black frame of the grid to support the gauze; the black also helps the metal gauze to stand out. Place a piece of parchment on the Easy-Grid Regular Mesh. Stick the parchment onto the wire or onto the black frame with medical adhesive tape (this adheres better to metal than normal adhesive tape).

2 Take up the "Diamond" perforating tool and slide the square point into the grid beside the parchment. The point will take up a position which is square with the mazes. Hold the tool in this position (do not turn it) and move it to the place where you want to begin perforating.

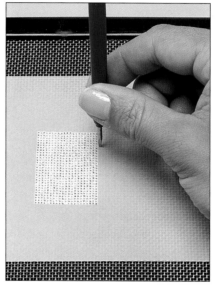

3 Hold the tool vertically, place it over an open square of the grid, and punch gently. The point will penetrate the parchment until the grid stops it. Perforate the pattern as indicated on template BT5-1 in this way, counting the holes carefully. Perforating in two steps, shallow and deep, is not applicable when using the Easy-Grid.

4 Practice this technique again. Paint a square onto the reverse side of a piece of parchment using Tinta white ink. Place the parchment on the Easy-Grid, making sure that the border of the square runs parallel to the gauze. Perforate a pattern as indicated in template BT5-2, using the same tool. Skip four holes between each four-hole design. It is best to perforate in rows from left to right working downward. Try to obtain an even result. If you want to perforate round holes instead of square holes use the "Arrow" tool.

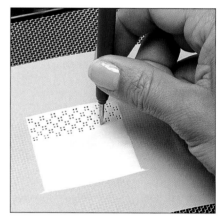

5 You can cut Easy-Grid perforations using the same cutting procedure as for 4-needle perforations (see page 15). There are many ways of cutting a perforated Easy-Grid pattern. In some of the projects in this book more elaborate perforating and cutting work (lace work) is applied.

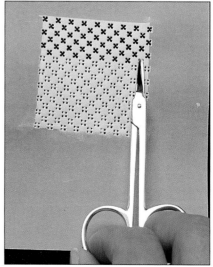

Painting with Perga-Color felt-tip pens

You will need
Mapping pen
Template BT6 (page 84)
Tinta ink: white 01T
Parchment paper, standard
Paintbrush no.2
Bowl of water
Pergamano sponge
Paper towel or tissue
Perga-Color Exclusive (PCE)
    felt-tip pens

1 Using a mapping pen, trace template BT6 with the Tinta white ink onto a piece of standard parchment paper. Before starting work, ensure that your brush is clean. Work your brush along your damp Pergamano sponge to moisten it. Remove any excess moisture by tapping the brush into a crumpled-up piece of paper towel or tissue.

2 Select PCE 12 and paint some dots along the outline of the butterfly.

3 Hold the brush in a flat position and spread the color in a circular motion. The tip of the brush should always point toward the outline of the area being painted (in this case toward the outline of the butterfly). Instead of turning your hand around, it is easier to turn the project as required in order to keep the tip of the brush pointing toward the outline.

The circular brush motion means you are pushing most of the color toward the outline of the area, fading out to the center. If you change color always clean your brush and moisten it on the sponge. Paint toward yourself using a counter-clockwise motion or away from yourself using a clockwise motion.

4 If you prefer, instead of putting dots on the outlines of the design you can take the color straight onto the tip of your brush from the Perga-Color felt-tip pen.

5 The finished result.

Painting with Tinta ink

You will need
Mapping pen
Template BT7 (page 84)
Tinta inks: white 01T, blue 02T
Parchment paper, standard
Paintbrush no.2
Saucer
Bowl of water
Paper towel

1 Using a mapping pen trace the template with Tinta white ink onto a piece of standard parchment paper. Put some droplets of white and blue Tinta ink on a saucer using the top of your brush. Clean the handle of the brush in water and dry it with paper towel.

2 First take a small amount of white ink onto the tip of the brush and then a small amount of blue. Because the darker color should always be on the tip of the brush it is always taken last. Apply the colors onto one of the flower petals using a dabbing movement. The brush should always point towards the outside of the petal so you will need to turn the project repeatedly. Hold the brush in an almost flat position. Continue to dab each petal until the brush has no more color on it. Rinse the brush in water, dry it on paper towel, then take some white followed by some blue ink onto the brush and continue painting.

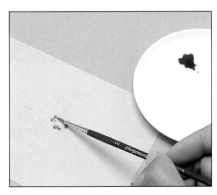

3 The result shows the blue color on the outer edges of the petals fading into lighter color toward the center. Dabbing is often used for flowers when more color depth is wanted.

Omitting traced outlines will often enhance the result of a painted design. Instead of tracing the design on the parchment first, you can paint the design with the template underneath, using the lines as a guide.

Painting with blended Tinta inks

You will need
Mapping pen
Template BT8 (page 84)
Parchment paper, standard
Tinta inks: light green 04T, blue 02T
Saucer
Paintbrush no.2
Bowl of water
Paper towel
Tinta ink: red 03T
Small ball embossing tool
HockeyStick embossing tool
"DeLuxe" embossing pad
Perga-Soft

1 Using a mapping pen, trace template BT8 onto a piece of parchment, using Tinta blue and green. Then put some droplets of Tinta green and Tinta blue on the saucer using the top of your brush.

First take a small amount of green onto the tip of the brush and then a small amount of blue. Paint a leaf, keeping the brush flat and working in a circular motion. The circular motion will blend the

two colors slightly and will give depth and structure to the leaf. Keep rinsing the brush in water and refilling the tip of the brush with Tinta green and blue respectively. Paint toward yourself in a counterclockwise motion or away from yourself using a clockwise motion.

2 Paint the strawberries with Tinta red, following the same motion described above. Paint the small leaves with Tinta green using a normal brush stroke. Your final result need not necessarily be the same as in this picture; leaves and strawberries in nature are often colored differently. If you want a stronger red around the outline of the strawberries repeat the painting process using the same circular motion after the first layer is dry. Finish by adding the white dots on the strawberries and emboss the flowers.

3 This picture shows the result after embossing. Embossing will highlight the colors; the white of the embossed parchment underneath the painted areas makes the colors lighter. The highlighting effect will be stronger in places where the ink layer is thin. Use the small ball embossing tool for the white petals and the strawberry leaves. Use the HockeyStick tool for the leaves and the outline of the strawberries.

Painting with Pintura paint

You will need
Mapping pen
Template BT9 (page 84)
Tinta inks: white 01T, light green 04T
Pintura paints: orange 05, brown 12,
    yellow 16, green 08
Parchment paper, standard
Saucer
Paintbrush no.2
Bowl of water
Paper towel
Pergamano sponge
Small, large ball embossing tools
HockeyStick embossing tool
"DeLuxe" embossing pad

1 Using a mapping pen, trace the lily design with Tinta white and light green onto a piece of parchment. Shake the bottles of Pintura orange, brown and yellow paint well, open them and put some droplets of each paint onto a saucer. Do not squeeze the bottle hard if you find the small opening has dried up: clean the opening with a paperclip or a needle and it should then open easily.

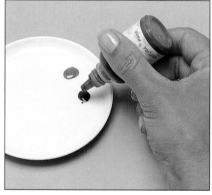

2 Rinse your brush in water, dry it on paper towel and drag it along a moist Pergamano sponge. Take a tiny bit of orange paint onto the tip of the brush. Remove any excess paint by rolling the brush between your fingers as you drag the brush across the saucer.

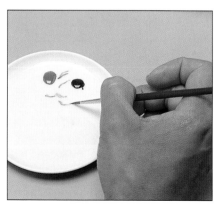

3 Color a petal of the lily, using a circular motion. The tip of the brush should always point toward the outline of the petal, pushing most of the color toward the outline, fading towards the center. Paint the center of the petals with Pintura yellow and the bud with Pintura orange.

4 Pintura paint dries rather quickly so you will need to rinse your brush in water at regular intervals. Dry it on paper towel then take a small amount of paint onto the tip of the brush again.

5 Using the tip of the brush, paint the stamens as very fine lines with Pintura brown. Paint the anthers of the stamens repeatedly in a darker orange. Paint the leaves by taking a tiny bit of Pintura yellow first and then a tiny bit of Pintura green onto the tip of the brush. Start the circular painting motion at the base of the leaf working along the outline.

6 This picture shows the result of the painted project before embossing. You can leave the picture like this or if you want to, you can emboss the design.

7 This image shows the highlighted result of embossing. On the reverse side of the design, lightly emboss the petals, leaves and bud using the HockeyStick tool.

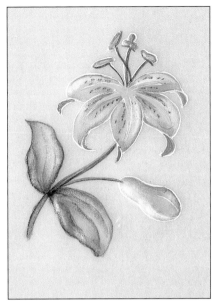

DESIGN INSPIRATION

Every craftsperson needs to find inspiration. It is a great idea to build up a scrapbook of creative designs that you can use for your parchment craft. Pictures of flowers, landscapes, animals, patterns, indeed anything that you might come across in books, magazines, or on a sheet of wrapping paper, can all inspire new ideas.

Some very skilled parchment crafters make their own lacy borders using crosshatched graph paper. It is important that the designed perforation template matches exactly with the dimensions of the perforating tools. The way around this is to use one of the Easy-Grids, then there is no need to draw perforating grids.

Gift Tags

H andmade parchment gift tags add a finishing touch to creatively wrapped gifts. These little folded cards, embossed in plain white or enhanced with gold, are just the right size for you to write the name of the recipient and a personal greeting inside.

The working sequence is the same for all the gift tags. Stick the parchment onto the template, making sure you have enough parchment for the front and back of the tag. When tracing with Tinta inks, remember to trace thin lines.

New Home

You will need

Parchment paper, standard
Templates (page 85)
Adhesive tape, non-permanent
Mapping pen
Tinta ink: white 01T
White pencil
Small ball embossing tool
"De Luxe" embossing pad
Perga-Soft
Piece of hard cardboard
1-needle perforating tool
"Excellent" perforating pad
Ruler
2-needle perforating tool
Pergamano scissors
Star-Tool
Ribbon
Tinta ink: gold 22T
HockeyStick embossing tool
4-needle perforating tool
Flower-Tool

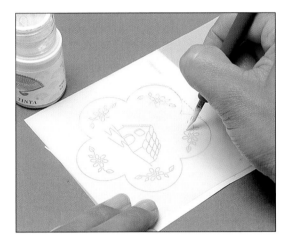

1 Trace the design using Tinta white ink and a mapping pen. Trace along the dashed folding line with white pencil.

2 Using the small ball embossing tool, lightly emboss the leaves, the door opening, the side of the house and the ground next to the footpath. Fully emboss the roof tiles, the flower petals, flower heart, the left part of the roof and between the double lines of the door opening and window.

3 Place the design on a piece of hard cardboard. On the reverse side of the design, stipple the door opening using the 1-needle tool.

4 Emboss the fold line using a ruler and the small ball tool.

5 Fold card. Place on perforating pad and perforate along the outline of the card using the 2-needle tool. Cut out the perforations using the Pergamano scissors.

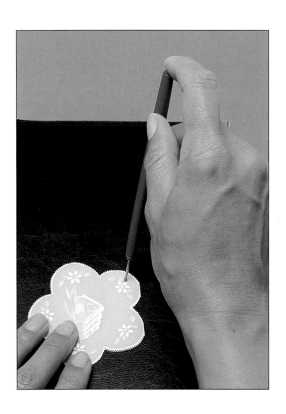

6 Make a small hole through both layers of the card using the Star-Tool. Place the embossing pad underneath the parchment and rotate the tool while applying gentle pressure. Thread a piece of ribbon through the hole.

Bear

Trace the outline of the hat, the ring around the planet, the nose, flower centers and rope using Tinta gold ink. Trace all the other lines using Tinta white. Lightly emboss the stars, moons and planet. Emboss the rope, nose, inside part of the collar, the ring around the planet and the white part of the eyes. Partially emboss the flower petals and flower centers. Emboss the ears, face and

outside part of the collar using the HockeyStick tool. Stipple the stars, moons and part of the planet using the 1-needle tool. Trace the fold using a white pencil and emboss it. Fold the card, perforate along the outline through the two layers using the 2-needle tool and cut out. Make a small hole in the card and thread a piece of ribbon through it.

Heart

Trace the double outline of the heart, inner heart and curved lines (with curly ends) using Tinta gold. Trace the flowers, small hearts, remaining curved lines and leaf shapes using Tinta white. Lightly emboss between double outline. Emboss flower petals, small hearts and part of the leaf shapes. Stipple between the double heart outline using the

1-needle tool. Trace the fold using a white pencil and emboss it. Fold the card and perforate along the outline using the 2-needle tool. Cut out 2-needle perforations. Make a small hole in the card through the two layers using the Star-Tool and thread a piece of ribbon through it. You might want to perforate the front page along the inner heart as well and cut this part out. This way you could write the recipient's initials inside the card.

Flower

Trace the entire design using Tinta white. Lightly emboss the stem and the leaves next to the flower. Using the HockeyStick tool, partly emboss the flower petals and the leaf shapes in the border. Emboss the stems in the border, the flower stamens and between the curved lines near the flower buds. Stipple the leaves and stem using the 1-needle tool. Trace the fold using a white pencil and emboss it. Fold the card and perforate along the outline using the 2-needle tool. Cut out the 2-needle perforations. Make a small hole through both layers of the card using the Star-Tool and thread a piece of ribbon through it.

Owl

Trace the double scalloped outline and the entire owl (apart from the short lines on its chest) using Tinta gold. Trace all remaining lines using Tinta white. Following the template perforate shallow using the 4-needle tool and the Flower-Tool. Lightly emboss the top of the head, the ears, around the eyes, the entire body, wings, leaves and claws. Emboss the beak, branch, legs, between the double lines in outline, the tear shapes in the corner decorations and the circles around the center holes of the Flower-Tool perforations. Stipple the top of the head, the ears and the wings. Repeat the perforations but do them deeply this time. Perforate deep using the 2-needle tool along the seven scallops near the fold and cut these perforations. Trace the dashed fold line using a white pencil and emboss it. Fold the card, perforate along the outline using the 2-needle tool and cut out. Make a small hole through both layers of the card using the Star-Tool and thread a piece of ribbon through it.

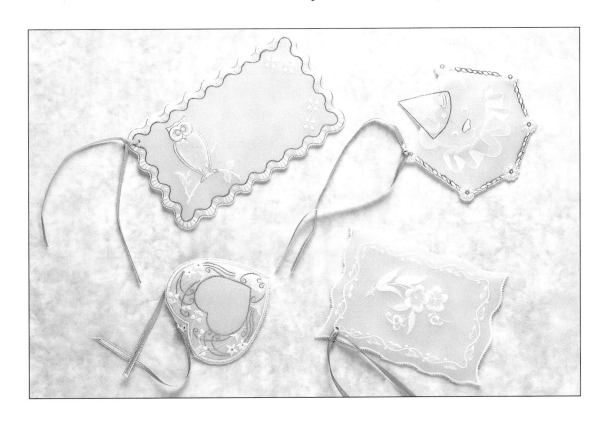

A gift of money will be all the more appreciated if it comes in an attractive handmade envelope! Because parchment is translucent, use a folded colored insert to hide the money until the recipient opens the envelope.

1 Position an entire parchment sheet on the template and stick it down with adhesive tape. Trace the decorative elements of the design with the mapping pen using Tinta gold ink.

You will need

Parchment paper, standard

Template (page 86)

Adhesive tape, non-permanent

Mapping pen

Tinta ink: gold 22T

Ruler

White pencil

"De Luxe" embossing pad

Extra small ball embossing tool

Perga-Soft

HockeyStick embossing tool

Hard, flat black cardboard

1-needle perforating tool

Paintbrush no.2

"Excellent" perforating pad

2-needle perforating tool

Pergamano scissors

Cutting mat and craft knife

Rainbow parchment or colored paper

Double-sided adhesive tape

2 Trace the folds and outline of the envelope design using a ruler and a white pencil. Take your time to ensure that your work is accurate.

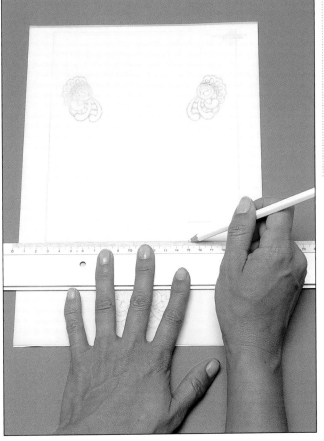

3 Place the project face-down on the embossing pad. Lightly emboss the large comma shapes and between the scalloped lines with the extra small ball tool. Finish off by embossing more heavily along the upper outline of the comma shapes using the HockeyStick tool.

4 Place the parchment onto the black cardboard. Using the 1-needle tool, stipple the small comma shapes inside the ovals and between the double lines underneath the oval (marked with "S" on the template). Emboss these areas lightly.

5 On the reverse side of the parchment color these areas that you have just worked on with white pencil.

artist's tip

Decorate the folded insert with one of the two smaller decorations from the design. You could also rule some decorative borders around the edges.

6 Using the paintbrush, paint between the straight and curved double lines using Tinta gold ink.

7 Place the work on the perforating pad and perforate using the 2-needle tool; the perforations are only partly indicated with dots in the template.

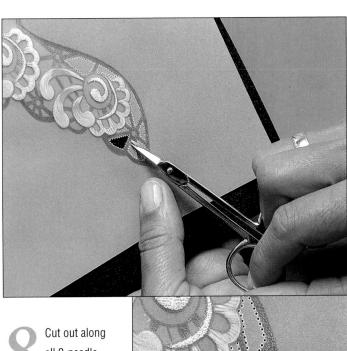

8 Cut out along all 2-needle perforations.

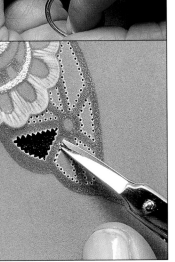

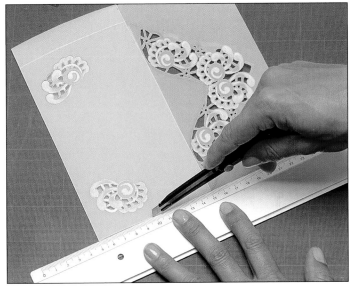

9 Emboss the folds and fold the envelope. Place onto a cutting mat and using a craft knife, cut both sides off straight. Cut a folded insert out of Pergamano Rainbow parchment or colored paper. Make this insert ¹⁄₁₆" (2 mm) smaller than the middle section of the envelope. Secure the flap of the envelope in place with a tiny piece of double-sided adhesive tape.

3

PROJECT

Birth
Announcement

Handmade parchment cards are a delightfully personal way with which to announce the birth of a baby. On receiving one of these announcements, like-minded friends may want to respond by making their own special greeting card. The idea of a matching card and envelope could be used for many special occasions.

1 Trace the single middle section of the dress (as indicated by figure B) with a mapping pen using Tinta-Pearl white. Apply Dorso lilac onto the bottom part of the dress (using a cotton bud for spreading). Emboss at front along folds of dress using the small ball tool. Perforate shallow along the hem using the Flower-Tool. Emboss the circle around the center hole of the Flower-Tool perforations. Perforate using the Flower-Tool again, but deep this time.

You will need

Parchment paper, standard
Template (page 87)
Mapping pen
Tinta-Pearl ink: white 01TP
Dorso Box 2
Cotton bud
Small ball embossing tool
"De Luxe" embossing pad
Perga-Soft
Flower-Tool
"Excellent" perforating pad
Lavender or eucalyptus oil
Paper towel or soft cloth
Tinta ink: white 01T
3-needle perforating tool
4-needle perforating tool
Easy-Grid Fine Mesh
Transparent adhesive tape, non-permanent
"Arrow" perforating tool
Pergamano scissors
2-needle perforating tool
Double-sided adhesive tape

2 Trace the front of the dress (indicated by figure A) using Tinta-Pearl white. Make sure there is enough parchment across the fold for the back of the dress (figure C). On the reverse of the design apply Dorso lilac behind the sleeves, on the collar and on the dress below the waistline. Put a spot of lavender or eucalyptus oil onto a piece of paper towel or a soft cloth and rub over the color gently.

3 Trace the outline of the back of the dress (indicated by figure C) on the reverse side using Tinta-Pearl white.

artist's tip
Make one card, including an envelope and an extra baby cap, have them photographed together with a printed announcement for a quick, yet very personal card.

4 Apply Tinta white on the reverse side of dress part A in the area above the waistline, indicated with the letter W. Place the project back onto the template.

5 With the template underneath, perforate shallow, using the 3- and 4-needle tools. Attach the project onto the Easy-Grid Fine Mesh at an angle of 45 degrees (half square) and fully perforate the part of the dress above the waistline indicated with W, using the "Arrow" perforating tool.

6 Emboss small dots inside the 4-needle perforations, fully emboss the flower petals and between the double lines in the sleeves and in the bottom part of the dress. Lightly emboss the ribbons and collar. Perforate 3- and 4-needle perforations again, but deep this time. Twist the 3-needle tool gently from left to right and the three holes will become oval-shaped.

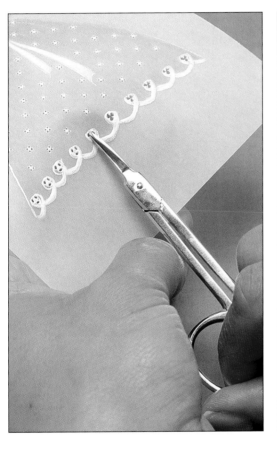

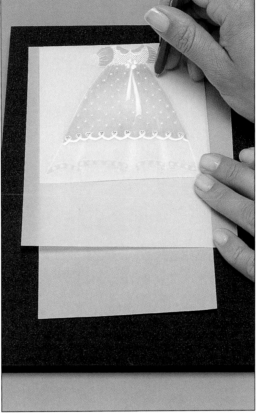

7 Cut open the 3-needle perforations. Emboss the fold line on the reverse side with the small ball tool.

8 Fold the card; attach the (single) middle section inside the folded card using non-permanent transparent tape. Perforate along the outline through all three layers of parchment using the 2-needle tool. Cut out all three layers of the project along the 2-needle perforations. Attach the single card back inside the folded card using double-sided adhesive tape.

9 To make the envelope trace the template, color it with Dorso lilac, perforate and emboss it. Trace the folds, fold the envelope and use double-sided adhesive tape for the glue strips.

4 PROJECT Greeting Card

In China, fish images mean "may you have sufficient food for tomorrow" or, more generally, "good luck". You will notice fish depicted on many Oriental greeting cards, paintings, writing paper and so on. The lacy border in this project can be used in many other card designs. Swap the templates inside the rectangular outline for another design in this book (for example see gallery on page 40).

1 Place the template underneath the parchment and fix in place with adhesive tape. Position the template to the right-hand side of the paper, making sure that there is enough paper on the left-hand side for the back of the card. Trace the seaweed using Tinta leaf green.

You will need

Template (page 88)
Parchment paper, standard
Adhesive tape, non-permanent
Mapping pen
Tinta ink: leaf green 10T
Tinta-Pearl yellow 16TP, red 03TP
Saucer
Paintbrush no. 2
Tinta ink: gold 22T
White pencil
Ruler
Dorso Box 1
Lavender or eucalyptus oil
Paper towel or soft cloth
Easy-Grid Fine Mesh
"Excellent" perforating pad
"Arrow" perforating tool
Small ball embossing tool
"De Luxe" embossing pad
Perga-Soft
HockeyStick embossing tool
Pergamano scissors
2-needle perforating tool

2 Put a spot of Tinta-Pearl yellow and Tinta-Pearl red onto a saucer and mix together with the brush. Using a circular movement, use this color to paint the fish. The tip of the brush should always point toward the outlines, pushing most of the color toward them.

P R O J E C T

3 Trace the scalloped outline of the card and apply details to the fish using Tinta gold. Lightly trace the fold and outline of the card using a white pencil and ruler.

4 On the reverse of the project, apply Dorso turquoise along the inside of the scalloped border. Put a spot of lavender or eucalyptus oil onto a piece of paper towel or a soft cloth and rub over the color gently.

5 Attach the project onto the Easy-Grid Fine Mesh and, following perforating pattern A, perforate the area marked A using the "Arrow" perforating tool.

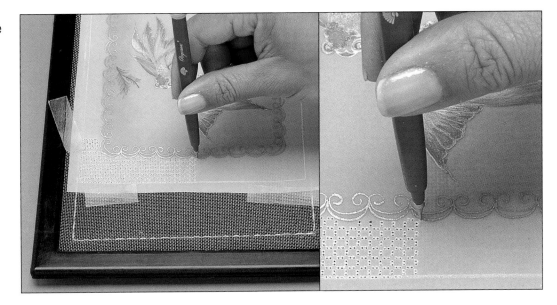

6 Using the small ball tool, emboss the dots inside the Easy-Grid perforations, between the scalloped lines and on the card outline. Emboss the fish details using the HockeyStick. Trace the double card outline using Tinta gold and paint between these lines using Tinta gold.

7 Cut out the Easy-Grid perforations. Fold the card and perforate along its outline, through both layers, using the 2-needle tool. Cut out the card along the 2-needle perforations.

A special occasion warrants a special card. Use this as a wedding invitation, announcement, or the outer cover for a printed order of service. The golden rings and heart can be traced on the card or can both feature as three-dimensional elements glued on top of each other. The dashed heart on the template marks the position of this three-dimensional element so do not trace over it. You can also enlarge the heart by 200 per cent so it is twice the size. Draw the fold at the top and you have a perfect Valentine or similar greeting card.

You will need

Parchment paper, standard
Template (page 88)
Adhesive tape, non-permanent
Ruler
White pencil
Mapping pen
Tinta ink: white 01T, gold 22T
Dorso Box 1
Lavender or eucalyptus oil
Paper towel or soft cloth
4-needle perforating tool
"Excellent" perforating pad
Small ball embossing tool
"De Luxe" embossing pad
Perga-Soft
2-needle perforating tool
Pergamano scissors
5-needle perforating tool
HockeyStick embossing tool
Paintbrush no.2
Pergakit glue

1 Trace the fold, using a white pencil. Trace the scalloped heart, the petals in the corners and all the little flowers around the heart using Tinta white ink.

2 Trace the small dots above the heart, the central dots in the corners and the stalks using Tinta gold. Apply Dorso blue on the reverse side around the heart. Put a spot of lavender or eucalyptus oil onto a piece of paper towel or a soft cloth and rub over the color gently.

3 Place the design back onto the template. Perforate the corners shallow, using the 4-needle tool.

4 Fully emboss the flower petals, leaves, fold line, the dots around the heart and the remaining dots in the corners. Lightly emboss the scalloped lines along the corner outlines and the heart shape.

artist's tip

This card could be used for all manner of occasions if you do not incorporate the heart and ring design into it. Write a personal greeting or an announcement on the front instead.

5 Perforate deep, using the 4-needle tool. Perforate along the scalloped outlines of the corners using the 2-needle tool. Cut the 4-needle perforations into crosses and slits. Cut out the 2-needle perforations along the corners at the fold.

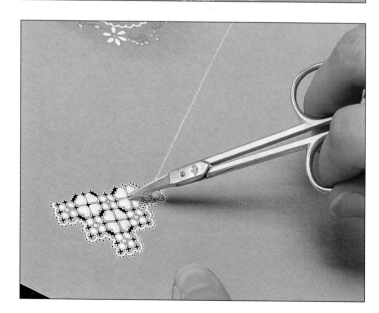

6 Fold the card (do not fold the protruding part of the corner decorations). Attach the project to the template and perforate shallow along the straight outlines using the 5-needle tool. Emboss the circle around the center of the 5-needle perforations. Perforate again using the 5-needle tool, but deeply this time. Cut out the card along the outer holes of the 5-needle perforations.

7 Trace the three-dimensional part of the heart shape using Tinta white ink. Perforate shallow along the outline of the heart using the 5-needle tool. Emboss lightly along the inside of the heart using the HockeyStick tool. Emboss the small circles around the central hole of the 5-needle perforations. Perforate deep along the outline of the heart. Cut the heart out along the outer holes of the perforations.

8 Trace and paint the rings using Tinta gold ink. Using the small ball tool emboss the design and then perforate around the outside edge using the 2-needle tool. Cut out.

9 Using Pergakit, attach the three-dimensional heart onto the card, then glue the rings on top of the heart.

Lily Greeting Card
Use the border from the Greeting Card (template on page 88) and the lily design (template BT9 on page 84). In this example, we have increased the size of the lily design by 145%. Use Pintura paints for painting the lily. There are endless possibilities for creating unique cards by combining different borders and designs.

Valentine Card
Enlarge the Gift Tags/Heart template (see page 85) by 170%. Trace the design in white. Use the Easy-Grid Fine Mesh and the Arrow tool to perforate. Cut a rectangle of parchment 11" x 5" (28 x 12 cm) and fold in half. Affix a single card inside this one, on which you can write a message. Fix the heart to the front of the card. Flowers and leaves are 3-D parchment (3005 and 3006).

Gift-wrap
Use Rainbow parchment. Using a white pencil mark the front dimensions of the box to be wrapped on the parchment. Leave enough parchment on all sides for wrapping. Decorate the front with some lace work and embossed lines. Finish with a ribbon and a bow. Decorate the front with three 3-D ready-colored parchment flowers (3008).

Celebration
Gallery

Gift Boxes
These pretty boxes are made from the Gift Box template (see page 91), although there is much less cutting and perforating to do. Choose Rainbow or even Fantasy parchment and change the lace work for decoration B (template on page 91). Refer to the Gift Box project on page 58, for tracing, embossing and assembly instructions.

Scroll
Take an A4 sheet of standard parchment and color it with yellow-ochre Dorso. Keeping 1½" (4 cm) free at both sides, draw straight gold lines, parallel to the short side of the sheet. Write your message on these lines. Tear irregular pieces from the paper, about ½" to 1" (1 to 3 cm) wide from all sides. Color the torn edges with Tinta gold. Roll up the paper and secure with gold cord. Make a loose 3-D decoration from the Gift Envelope template (page 86) and affix it with Pergakit glue.

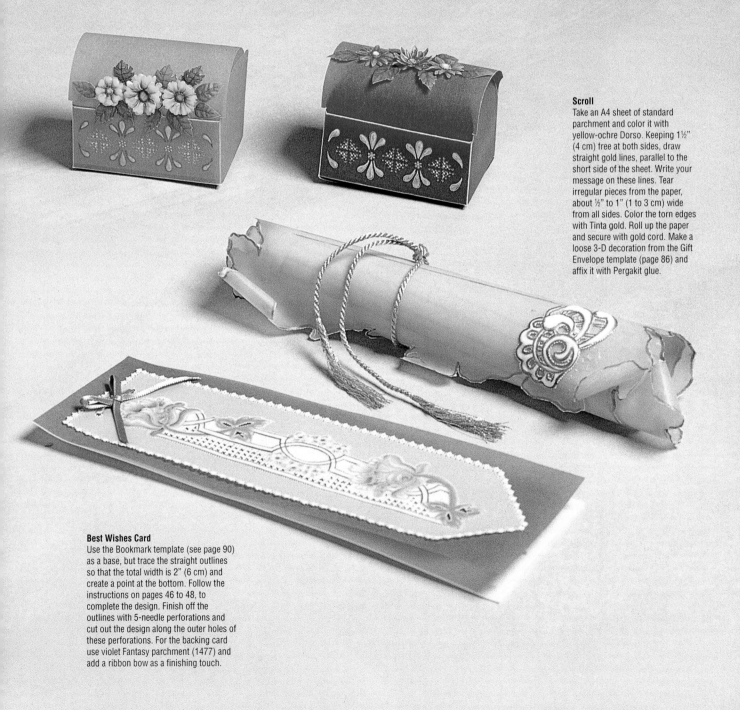

Best Wishes Card
Use the Bookmark template (see page 90) as a base, but trace the straight outlines so that the total width is 2" (6 cm) and create a point at the bottom. Follow the instructions on pages 46 to 48, to complete the design. Finish off the outlines with 5-needle perforations and cut out the design along the outer holes of these perforations. For the backing card use violet Fantasy parchment (1477) and add a ribbon bow as a finishing touch.

Parasol Mobile

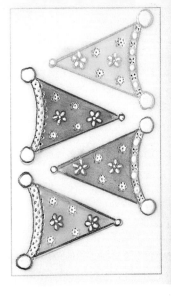

This delicately colored eight-parasol parchment mobile is a pretty addition to any room. The parasols can also be used as decorations for gifts, menu cards or even the top of a festive cake. They also make attractive place cards.

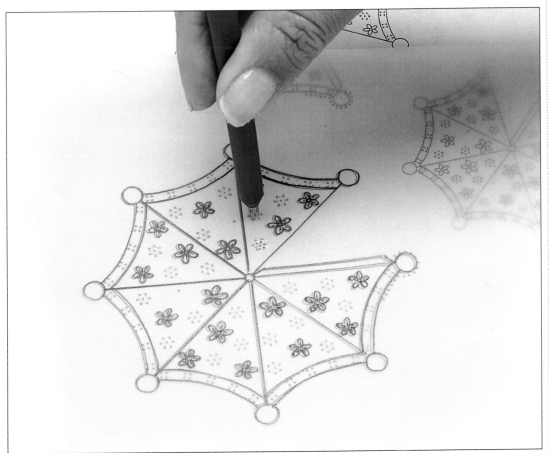

You will need

Parchment paper, standard

Templates (page 89)

Adhesive tape, non-permanent

Mapping pen

Tinta ink: white 01T, light green 04T

Tinta-Pearl blue 02TP, red 03TP, yellow 16TP

Dorso Box 1

Lavender or eucalyptus oil

Paper towel or soft cloth

"Flower-Tool" perforating tool

4-needle perforating tool

5-needle perforating tool

"Excellent" perforating pad

Small ball embossing tool

"De Luxe" embossing pad

Perga-Soft

2-needle perforating tool

Pergamano scissors

Ruler

Small craft scissors

Paper glue

Wooden sticks with pointed ends

Craft knife

Cutting mat

1-needle perforating tool

Sixteen pearl beads, fourteen 5 mm and two 7 mm

Soft thread

Semi-Star perforating tool

Four-in-Four perforating tool

1 Prepare the templates as instructed on page 89. The single segment shows a different design idea for the border (steps 2 and 3 on page 44 show this in detail). Trace the templates as follows: template A four times, B twice and C once, using Tinta at random (Tinta-Pearl blue, Tinta-Pearl red, Tinta-Pearl yellow and a combination of Tinta-Pearl blue and Tinta light green). Color the designs on the reverse side with Dorso light green, yellow and magenta at random. Put a spot of lavender or eucalyptus oil onto a piece of paper towel or a soft cloth and rub over the color gently. Perforate the six small parasols shallow using the Flower-Tool, 4-needle tool or 5-needle tool depending on the template you are using. Note that since this is an enlarged pattern, the tools will not fit. Use the perforations in the pattern as an indication as to where to perforate.

2 Variation with 4-needle tool: emboss the small and large dots, the little flowers and the circle around the center hole of the Flower-Tool perforations on the reverse side. Perforate deep using the Flower-Tool and the 4-needle tool and use the 2-needle tool for the outline of the parasol. Cut the 4-needle perforations into crosses and cut the outline along the 2-needle perforations.

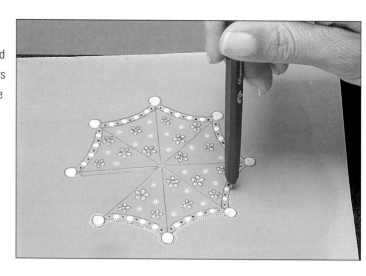

3 Variation with 5-needle tool: emboss the small and large dots, the little flowers and the small circle around the center hole of the Flower-Tool and every second 5-needle perforation. Cut the outline along the outer holes of the 5-needle perforations and 2-needle perforations around large dots.

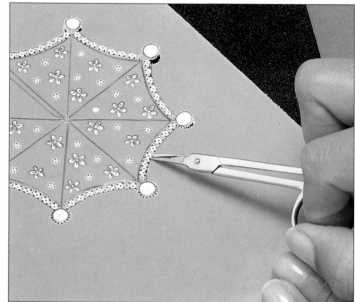

4 Cut out the V-shape using small craft scissors. On the reverse side emboss the parasol folds using a ruler and the small ball embossing tool.

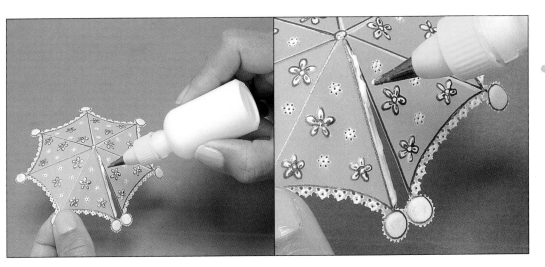

5 Stick the two edges together with paper glue.

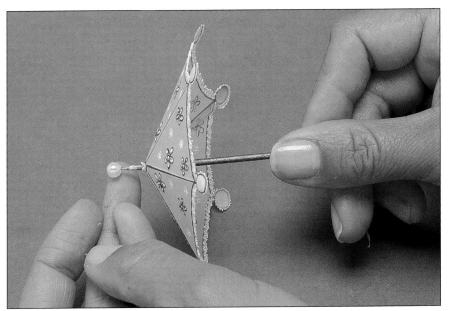

6 Cut the wooden sticks to a length of about 3" (8 cm) and color them with Tinta-Pearl inks. To create a groove in the blunt end of the stick, place the stick on the cutting mat, position the knife slightly in from the end of the stick, at a right angle to it and roll the stick around, gently pressing the knife into it. Perforate a hole in the center of the parasols using the 1-needle tool; apply paper glue to the inside of the parasols and slide the pointed end of the sticks through the hole. Apply a small dot of glue to the top of the stick and place a pearl on it.

7 Tie a piece of soft thread around the groove on the end of the stick. Twist the two ends around each other, apply a little glue and insert the thread through the pearl. Make all the remaining parasols following the above instructions. Trace and make parasol D (see page 89). Use the Semi-Star perforating tool on the center of the Flower-Tool dots. Perforate once, rotate the tool half a turn (180 degrees) and perforate again, sliding the five needles in the same holes to complete the stars (it's a good idea to practice doing this on a scrap piece of parchment first). Use the Four-in-Four perforating tool in the border on the spots of the 4-needle dots; cut the four center holes to crosses. Emboss this parasol in exactly the same way as the smaller ones. Insert a stick into the large parasol, glue it at the top and reinforce it with a round piece of parchment (approximately 1"/2.5 cm diameter) in the top. Glue on the large beads. Assemble mobile by hanging the small parasols at different lengths with thin soft thread from the seven round corners of the large parasol.

B ooks and parchment share a long and happy history. In medieval times, scribes copied books onto real parchment. This pretty bookmark would be a wonderful gift for someone who loves books and would never dream of folding over the corner of a page.

1 Look carefully at the photograph of the finished bookmark; trace the appropriate parts of the design in gold, then trace the rest of the template using Tinta-Pearl white.

2 Paint the large flower at the top of the design using your brush and PCE pen no. 10. For the large flower at the bottom use PCE pen no. 5.

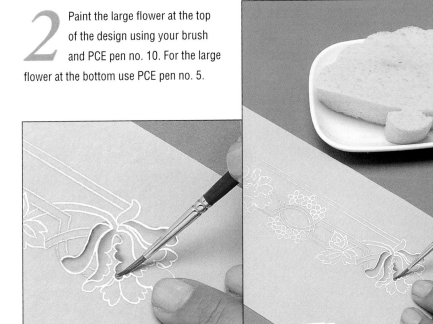

You will need

Parchment paper, standard
Template (page 90)
Adhesive tape, non-permanent
Mapping pen
Tinta ink: gold 22T
Tinta-Pearl white 01TP
Pergamano sponge
Paintbrush no.2
Perga-Color Exclusive (PCE) felt-tip pens
"De Luxe" embossing pad
Small ball embossing tool
HockeyStick embossing tool
Perga-Soft
Medical adhesive tape
Easy-Grid Fine Mesh
"Excellent" perforating pad
"Arrow" perforating tool
Easy-Grid Regular Mesh
"Diamond" perforating tool
2-needle perforating tool
Pergamano scissors
Rainbow pastel or fantasy parchment
Serrated scissors
Pergakit glue

parchment craft/project 7

3 Paint the petals of the small flowers at the sides using PCE 14 and the heart of the small flowers using PCE 3. Paint the stalks and between the double lines of the leaves using PCE 16.

4 Emboss the flower petals, between the straight double lines and the accents in the large flowers using the small ball tool and the HockeyStick tool.

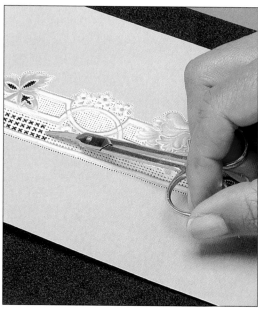

5 Using medical adhesive tape, attach the project faceup onto the Easy-Grid Fine Mesh and perforate the parts marked B using the "Arrow" perforating tool. Then attach the project onto the Easy-Grid Regular Mesh and perforate the parts marked A using the "Diamond" perforating tool. Perforate along the inside of the leaves and along the outlines of the bookmark using the 2-needle tool.

6 Cut along the 2-needle perforations inside the leaves. Cut the "Diamond" tool perforations into crosses. Cut out along the outlines of the bookmark.

artist's tip

These delicate bookmarks will last longer if they are covered in a clear sleeve. Specialty stationery/craft stores can make sleeves of clear plastic to your requirements. You could punch a hole through the sleeve and thread a piece of ribbon or a tassel through it.

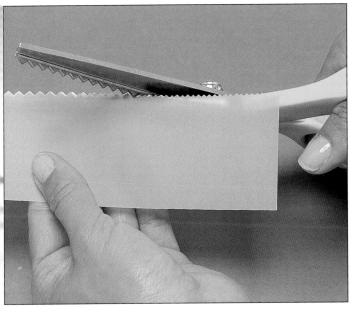

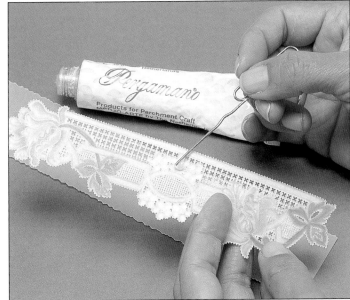

7 For the backing, cut a piece of Rainbow Pastel parchment 2" x 7" (5 x 18 cm). Cut along all four edges of the paper using serrated scissors. Cut over the edges again with the serrated scissors, to create a more delicate effect.

8 Using the end of a paperclip, lightly apply a layer of Pergakit glue over the embossed parts on the back of the bookmark. Position the bookmark centrally onto the colored parchment and stick in place.

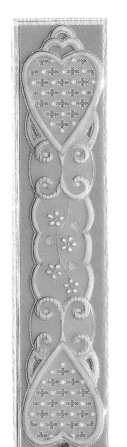

Alternative design

Book Fan

This bookmark is based on the fan design (template on page 90). To make the template for this design, make two photocopies of the fan template, cut both off straight 3¾" (9.5 cm) from the top. Line up the two parts and glue them onto a piece of normal paper. Do not worry that the flower design does not match up; trace only the outline from your new template, trace the flower design from the original fan template.

Alternative design

Delicate Marker

Trace the template on page 90 with white or colored Tinta-Pearl inks. Color the flowers using PCE 9 and 10. Using the 2-needle tool, perforate around the squares and flowers and use the Flower-Tool along the borders. Perforate areas marked "B" with Easy-Grid Fine Mesh and the Arrow tool. Emboss the white line, the circle around the center hole of the Flower-Tool perforations and parts marked "E" on the template. Cut out along the 2-needle perforations and outer holes of the Flower-Tool perforations. Attach a background of colored parchment and cut the edges with serrated scissors.

Mother's Day Rose Card

R oses are a good choice for Mother's Day and will be all
the more welcome if accompanied by this creative, handmade parchment greeting card. Painting the roses is
something of a challenge. Persevere until you achieve the
desired result.

You will need

Parchment paper, standard

Template (page 89)

Adhesive tape, non-permanent

Mapping pen

Tinta ink: white 01T

Tinta ink: gold 22T

Dorso Box 1

Lavender or eucalyptus oil

Paper towel or soft cloth

White pencil

Ruler

4-needle perforating tool

"Excellent" perforating pad

Semi-Circle perforating tool

Extra small ball embossing tool

"De Luxe" embossing pad

Perga-Soft

Pergamano scissors

Tinta inks: yellow 16T, red 03T, leaf green 10T, black 11T, violet 07T, blue 02T

Saucer

Paintbrush no.2

Craft knife

Serrated scissors

Gold thread

Pergamano Fantasy Parchment II, light green

Double-sided adhesive tape

1 This project consists of an outer folded card with lace work at the front, a folded insert with painted roses and a single green insert on which to write a message. Stick a sheet of parchment paper onto the template, allowing enough parchment to cover the back page across the fold. Trace the oval shapes in the corners using Tinta white. Trace the scalloped lines in the corners, the small dots, petals, stripes and ovals between the Semi-Circle perforations using Tinta gold. Apply Dorso yellow ochre on the reverse side along the inside of the scalloped lines (triangles). Put a spot of lavender or eucalyptus oil onto a piece of paper towel or soft cloth and rub over the color gently, it should fade out toward the semi-circle perforations. Trace the fold using a white pencil. Perforate shallow, using the 4-needle tool.

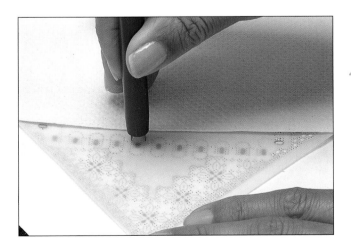

2 Perforate shallow using the Semi-Circle perforating tool.

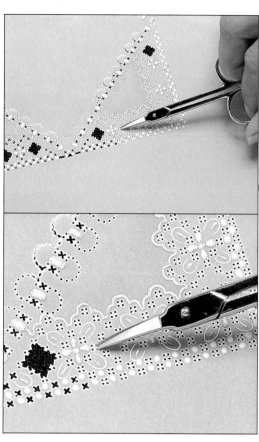

3 Using the extra small ball tool, emboss the ovals between the Semi-Circle perforations, small dots, petals and fold line. Perforate deep using the 4-needle and Semi-Circle tools.

4 Cut all 4-needle perforations in the corners as indicated in the enlarged detail on the template.

5 Stick a second sheet of parchment onto the template, allowing enough parchment across the fold for the back page. Do not trace the roses; the template is your guide for painting them.

Trace the fold using white pencil. Paint the roses and rosebuds: take a small amount of Tinta white, yellow and red (in this order) onto the brush. Paint in circular movements.

6 Paint the leaves and stem by taking a small amount of Tinta green, white and black (in this order) onto the brush. Paint in circular movements. To paint the small flowers, use Tinta violet for the petals, Tinta yellow for the flower hearts and Tinta black for the stamens.

7 Paint the bow by taking a small amount of Tinta white and blue onto the brush and painting in a circular movement. Apply darker detail with Tinta blue along the outline of the bow. Partly emboss the rose petals, bow, leaves and rosebuds. Fully emboss the petals and the heart of the small flowers and fold line. Finally, paint the gypsophila (using Tinta violet) and apply small dots at the end of these lines using Tinta white, by dabbing your brush on the parchment.

8 Fold both cards, slide into each other and trace the outlines of three layers on the reverse side, smaller than the outline of the front page using a ruler and white pencil. Cut off excess paper along the white line using a craft knife and ruler or serrated scissors. Cut along the outline perforations of the front page (see enlarged detail in template). Attach the folded card with the lacework using double-sided adhesive tape on the back page. Tie the two cards together with gold thread by simply putting the thread inside the card, up to the folded edge, bring the two thread ends to the front of the spine and tie a bow. Cut the folded green insert to size and attach it to the back page of the folded insert card with double-sided adhesive tape.

Fan

Fans, the epitome of elegance, femininity and beauty, have inspired many handmade parchment versions. The material and the perforating and cutting techniques are ideally suited to the production of a wide variety of delicate fans. You can also adapt the design to make a bookmark (see page 49).

1 Trace the template 12 times using Tinta white. Do not trace the parallel hatched lines or the crosshatched lines in the leaves.

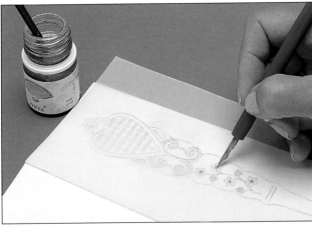

2 Clean your mapping pen and allow the white ink to dry. Carefully trace the center of the flowers with Tinta gold ink.

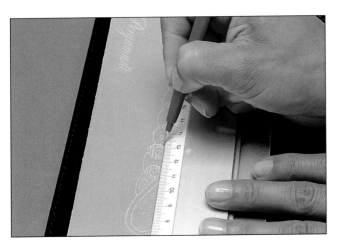

3 Perforate shallow using the 4-needle tool. On the reverse side, use the fine stylus embossing tool and a ruler to emboss the parallel hatched lines. At the front emboss the crosshatched fine lines in the little leaves using the 1-needle tool .

You will need

Parchment paper, standard

Template (page 90)

Adhesive tape, non-permanent

Mapping pen

Tinta ink: white 01T, gold 22T

4-needle perforating tool

"Excellent" perforating pad

Fine stylus embossing tool

"De Luxe" embossing pad

Perga-Soft

Ruler

1-needle perforating tool

White pencil

2-needle perforating tool

Pergamano scissors

Small craft scissors

19" (50 cm) ivory-colored ribbon, ⅟₁₆" (1.5 mm) wide

Craft glue

19" (50 cm) ivory-colored embroidery thread

4" (12 cm) silver embroidery thread

4 Emboss the petals, the hearts of the flowers and the dots between the 4-needle perforations.

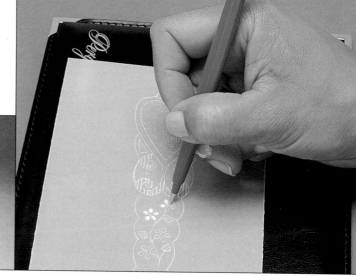

5 Using a white pencil color on the reverse side between the double lines of the heart shape and the curved ornaments at the top and sides of the heart shape. Delicately emboss these spaces on the reverse side.

6 Perforate all 4-needle perforations deep. Perforate all 2-needle perforations deep, as indicated in the template.

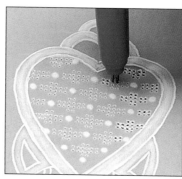

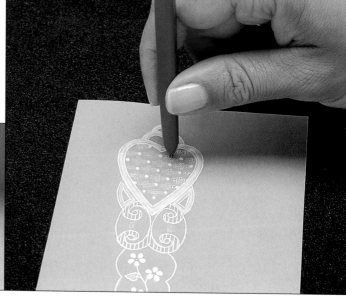

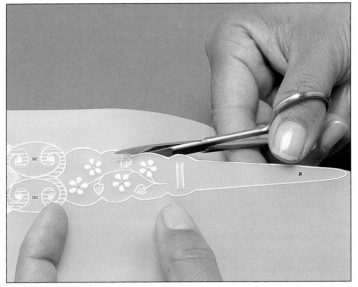

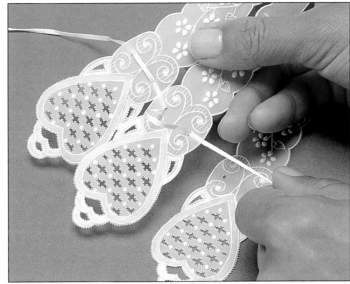

7 Cut all 2- and 4-needle perforations and the remaining perforations as shown in the template enlargement. Cut out the handle of the fan along the outline using small scissors.

8 Working on the reverse side, thread the ivory ribbon through the slits. Leave enough slack so that the fan will open properly. Leave a short piece of ribbon at each side. Fold the ends over and glue onto the back of the threaded ribbon.

Alternative design

Rainbow Fan

Trace the fan segment 12 times onto the soft color side of Rainbow Pastel Parchment. To create 12 segments with identical color patterning, you will need two identical sheets of parchment, which you will find in two packages (code 1484). Line up the tracing of the segments in such a way that they will be identical. Note that the embossed parts will show clear white at the front and will be highlighted at the back.

9 Wind the ivory and silver embroidery thread around four fingers and tie one end together by winding some thread around the bunch. Cut the other end. To attach to the fan, loosely thread a piece of embroidery thread several times through the holes in the handle parts and the top part of the tassel.

10 PROJECT Gift Box

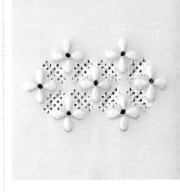

A special gift deserves a personal handmade parchment box. This tiny, delicately worked box will earn you much admiration for your creative skills. It could be filled with miniature soaps, fine chocolates or candies.

You will need

Parchment paper, standard
Template (page 91)
Adhesive tape, non-permanent
White pencil
Ruler
Mapping pen
Tinta ink: white 01T, gold 22T
4-needle perforating tool
"Excellent" perforating pad
Small ball embossing tool
"De Luxe" embossing pad
Perga-Soft
Pergamano scissors
Small craft scissors
Pergakit glue

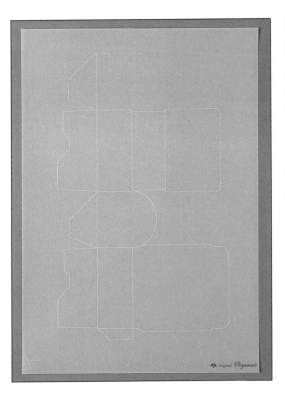

1 Trace the folds and outlines of the entire gift box with a white pencil. Take your time to ensure that your work is accurate.

2 Trace the little petals with Tinta white and the flower hearts with Tinta gold.

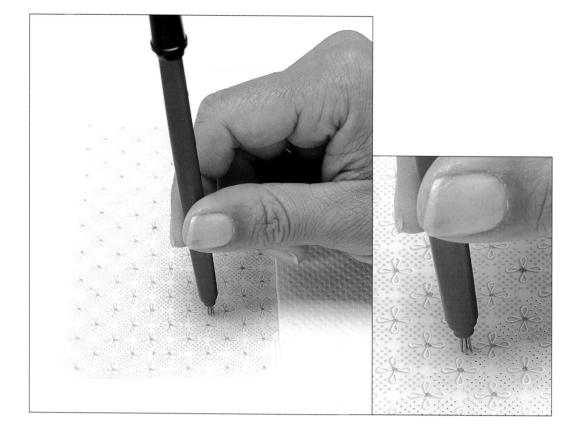

3 Perforate shallow using the 4-needle tool as indicated in the template.

4 Emboss the petals using the small ball tool.

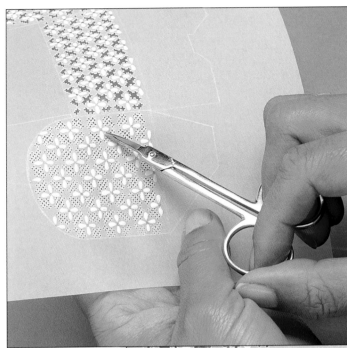

5 Perforate all 4-needle perforations deep. Using the small ball embossing tool and a ruler, emboss the fold lines, taking care to emboss on the correct side (see template instructions). Fold the box along the folds, unfold it again and gently flatten the folds. You need to fold the box before cutting the crosses and slits to prevent any damage to the project. The parchment will weaken through cutting.

6 Cut 4-needle perforations as shown in the enlargement on the template.

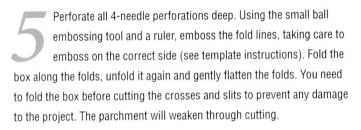

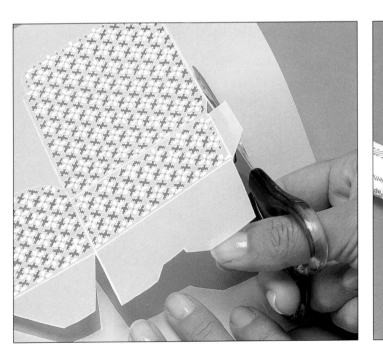

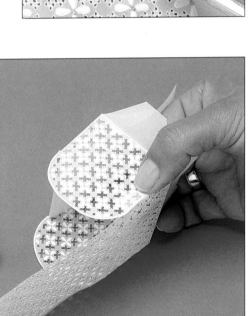

7 Cut out the box along the outline using small craft scissors.

8 Carefully fold the box again. Glue the sides of the box together using Pergakit.

Home Decoration
Gallery

Picture Frame

To make the template you will need a set square. A small A3 size drawing board with a set-square on a rail is useful. Draw the inner double rectangular shape of the frame; copy the Gift Envelope flap twice (template on page 86), cut out and position them at opposite corners of the rectangle. Complete the template by drawing the double outlines. Trace the template on white parchment leaving enough parchment on all sides to fit underneath the mount. Fill the "empty" areas with a perforation design as used in the border of the Greeting Card (pattern on page 88).

Napkin Rings

Make the small parasols in exactly the same way as shown on pages 42 to 45. In order to create the ring, flexible thread covered with colored plastic should be used, this is available in most craft stores. Using Pergakit glue, affix the parasol to one end of a 6" (15 cm) length of flexible plastic thread. Wrap the thread around the napkin.

Tablemats

Make a template by drawing a circle with a diameter of 6" (15 cm). Position four ½" (1.1 cm) wide and 1¼" (3.2 cm) long strips of the lace work of the Gift Box (pattern on page 91) around the circle, one at the top, one at 90°, one at 180°, etc. Use template BT7 to add one flower design between the lace work. Copy the template onto white parchment, perforate and cut the lace work. Finish the outline with 5-needle perforations and cutting. Use a slightly larger circle of colored parchment as a background so that the lace work stands out. Have the project sealed between two layers of clear plastic to protect it from dust and moisture.

Cylindrical Lampshade

Use a full sheet of lilac Fantasy Parchment (1477). Take an A4 sheet of graph paper and draw five pairs of lines, approximately 2" (6 cm) long and ¼" (6 mm) apart at the top of the sheet, parallel to the short side of the paper. Similarly, draw four pairs of lines at the bottom of the paper. Divide the lines equally across the sheet. Mark where you want the 5-needle perforations in between the lines. Copy the template onto your sheet of lilac Fantasy Parchment using Tinta gold. Perforate with the 5-needle tool between the double lines and cut these out. Perforate stars at random using the Semi-Star tool and cut the inner perforations with Pergamano scissors. You might decide to finish the top border of the shade with a double gold line. The nightlight must be in a holder and it is very important to cut air vent openings at the bottom of the shade to prevent the candle from smoking. Lit candles must never be left unattended.

Menu Card

You could use any of the patterns and designs in this book to decorate a menu card. Make the outer card from standard white parchment. Cut an insert card to size, to write the menu on. Alternatively, you could use a computer and print the menu in an elegant font onto a sheet of parchment or ordinary paper and insert it in the card.

Personalized Placecards

These placecards are simple and quick to make and add that personal touch. Use Tinta gold to trace the Gift Tag/Owl template on page 85. Emboss the white details as shown and write in the name of your guest.

11 PROJECT Lampshade

In the past, lampshades were often made out of real parchment. Being rigid and translucent, it allowed the light to shine through. The parchment we use today has similar properties; it can be used for small and medium-sized lampshades and can be decorated with perforation work and three-dimensional elements. Choose a frame or wine glass on which to place the shade. Because the perforating is done with the Easy-Grid, it is possible to adapt the size of the template to fit any shade or glass.

1 Trace the template with Tinta white and gold ink (look carefully at the photograph of the finished item to see what should be traced in each color).

2 Trace 12 separate flowers using Tinta white and gold inks.

3 Color the template on the reverse side with Dorso blue, leaving the triangles at the bottom and the glue strip free. Put a spot of lavender or eucalyptus oil onto a piece of paper towel or a soft cloth and rub over the color gently. Remove any excess Dorso with a clean cotton bud moistened with a drop of lighter fluid. Intensify the color of the flowers by applying Dorso blue on the front using a cotton bud.

You will need

Parchment paper, standard
Template (page 92)
Adhesive tape, non-permanent
Mapping pen
Tinta ink: white 01T, gold 22T
Dorso Box 1
Lavender or eucalyptus oil
Paper towel or soft cloth
Cotton buds
Lighter fluid
Small ball embossing tool
"De Luxe" embossing pad
Perga-Soft
Easy-Grid Fine Mesh
"Excellent" perforating pad
"Arrow" perforating tool
2-needle perforating tool
Straight-Four perforating tool
Small craft scissors
Pergakit glue
Pergamano scissors
Craft knife
Ruler
Double-sided adhesive tape

4 Using the small ball tool, emboss the separate three-dimensional flowers, between the double-lined outlines and the scalloped lines and gold dots.

5 Perforate the triangles marked "A" at the bottom with the Easy-Grid Fine Mesh and the "Arrow" tool. Perforate according to pattern A on page 92. (You can also use the Easy-Grid Regular Mesh and the "Diamond" tool).

6 Perforate along the inner and outer outline of the lampshade, using the 2-needle tool or Straight-Four tool.

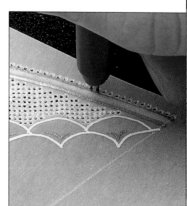

artist's tip

Draw the basic outline of the lampshade on a sheet of Fantasy parchment of your choice. Affix small, identical 3-D flowers (either ones you have made yourself, or pre-printed color ones, product 3008) in a regular pattern on the outside and you have a quick and easy lampshade.

7 Cut out the three-dimensional flowers using craft scissors and stick them onto the project using small dots of Pergakit glue. Using the Pergamano scissors, cut out the outline of the lampshade along the 2-needle perforations.

8 Cut the two edges using craft scissors or a craft knife along the edge of a ruler. Attach double-sided adhesive tape to one edge.

9 Form the lamp into its conical shape and press the edges together firmly so that the tape adheres. Dorso color on the inside of the glue strip can prevent the tape from adhering properly. Clean it with a cotton bud moistened with a drop of lighter fluid. Test your lighter fluid first for this purpose.

Alternative design

Rainbow lamp

Select an A4 sheet of Rainbow Pastel parchment (1484), or you might select an evenly colored and rigid Fantasy Parchment sheet. In this alternative, the Easy-Grid perforations have been left out.

12

PROJECT

Picture Border

A delicate parchment frame provides an unusual and attractive way with which to display photographs and other mementos of sentimental value. The finished project is perforated and cut along the scalloped outline of the parchment. A photograph is placed behind the border and mounted onto a sheet of colored paper. Clear non-reflecting glass or artificial glass display the border to best effect.

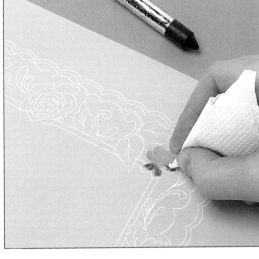

1 Position a sheet of parchment over the template and fix in place with adhesive tape. Trace the entire template using Tinta white ink.

2 Apply a little color using the Dorso crayons to one of the flowers. Fold a piece of paper towel into a firm tip, put a spot of lavender or eucalyptus oil onto it and use this to spread the color evenly across the surface of the flower. Repeat this process to color the remaining flowers – two purple, two fuschia pink and one yellow. Color the roses red.

3 Working on the reverse side of the design, use the fine stylus embossing tool to emboss the outline of the petals of the five small flowers. Hold the tool at an angle and start the fine lines at the outside edge of the petals.

You will need

Parchment paper, standard
Template (page 93)
Adhesive tape, non-permanent
Mapping pen
Tinta ink: white 01T
Dorso box 1
Dorso box 2
Paper towel
Lavender or eucalyptus oil
Fine stylus embossing tool
Large ball embossing tool
"De Luxe" embossing pad
Perga-Soft
HockeyStick embossing tool
1-needle perforating tool
Hard, black cardboard
"Diamond" perforating tool
Easy-Grid Regular Mesh
2-needle perforating tool
"Excellent" perforating pad
Scissors or craft knife
Adhesive tape
Double-sided adhesive tape
Sheet of colored paper
Frame

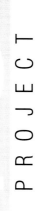
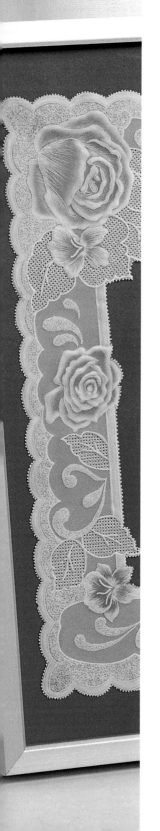

4 Draw very short, fine lines from the center of the petals to give the flowers texture. Emboss between the double scalloped outline and the double straight lines using the large ball embossing tool.

5 Emboss the large and small roses along the outlines of all the petals using the large ball embossing tool and the HockeyStick tool. Try to create a clear white coloring at the rim, fading to a greyish-white toward the inside of the petal.

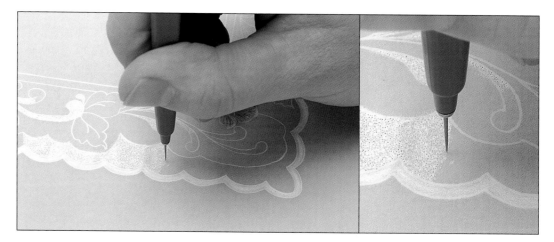

6 Using the 1-needle tool, stipple the area just inside the scalloped border (marked B on the template) and the long comma shapes. This is quite a large area to work on; if the stippling is too dense the parchment will look white and it may bubble because of the stretching effect. Experiment on some scrap pieces of parchment first to decide what effect you want to create.

7 Perforate the leaves with the Diamond perforating tool and use the Easy-Grid, regular mesh. You can decide whether to position the design square on to the grid or at a 45° angle. If you place the design at an angle, the perforated lines in the leaves will run diagonally.

8 Perforate the design along the outer and inner edge using the 1- or 2-needle tool. Cut out along these perforations.

9 Make a photocopy of the template and using scissors or a craft knife cut out the central space where the photograph will be placed. Position your chosen photograph behind this paper template and affix with tape. Cut the photograph to the required shape and size following the outer straight lines of the inside border. Now fix the photograph to the parchment border using double-sided adhesive tape.

10 The sheet of colored paper is used as the mount, so should be cut to fit the frame. Stick the photo with the parchment border to the mount using four tiny dots of Pergakit glue placed underneath the embossed areas. Position inside the frame.

This traditional Victorian-style village winter scene of a church tower and small cottages with snow-covered roofs will appeal to many. Dorso crayons are used to maximum effect and a three-dimensional element adds to the originality of this design.

1 Attach a sheet of parchment onto the template, allowing enough parchment for the front page across the folding line. Trace the back page of the card on the right-hand side of the sheet. Trace the trees, the snow on the roofs and on the ground using Tinta-Pearl white. Trace the walls of the houses using Tinta sepia. Apply bands of Dorso above the landscape working from bottom to top using yellow, orange, purple, blue and back to purple. Put a spot of lavender or eucalyptus oil onto a piece of paper towel or a soft cloth and rub over the color gently.

2 Paint the pine trees using Pinta-Perla green. Using Tinta-Pearl white for the snow, paint the roofs and the relevant parts of the pine trees; Pintura white and a little Pintura cinnamon for the church and five houses; Pintura yellow for the windows and Pintura brown for the brick wall.

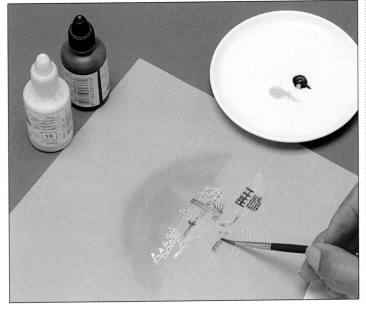

3 Emboss the snow on the ground using the HockeyStick embossing tool. Also use this tool and the large ball embossing tool to emboss the snow on the roofs and trees.

4 Place the painted landscape faceup onto the template and mark out the two points indicated "F" in the template using a white pencil. Remove the project from the template, turn the project over, place back on the template and line up the two "F" marks (the landscape is now facedown). Attach the project to the template. Trace the fold along a ruler using a white pencil.

artist's tip

To create a slightly different card, instead of perforating the areas marked "A" in the template, use Dorso color. This is a quick way of making this card, if you have lots of Christmas greetings to send.

5 Trace the front page using Tinta gold for the card outline; Tinta-Pearl white for the small scalloped lines around the perforations and the snow on the lantern; Tinta leaf green for the holly; Tinta red for the berries; Tinta sepia for the lantern, candle and flame. Trace the lantern a second time on a scrap piece of parchment (this is used for the three-dimensional element).

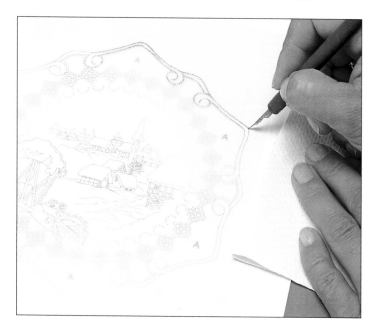

6 Paint the front page. Use Pinta-Perla green and a little Pintura green for the holly; Pintura red and a little Pintura bordeaux for the berries and Pintura white for the shiny spot on the berries. Paint the three-dimensional lantern using Pintura cinnamon and a little Pintura grey. Use Pintura white and a little Tinta-Pearl white for the snow on the lantern; Tinta gold for the candle and Pintura orange for the flame.

7 Perforate shallow using the 4-needle tool (not along the outline) and deep using the Semi-Circle tool, following the template. Emboss the dots inside the 4-needle perforations, the holly and the berries. Lightly emboss between the double outline using the HockeyStick tool. Perforate using the 4-needle tool again, but deep this time. Attach the project to the Easy-Grid Fine Mesh and perforate the parts

marked "A" on the template using the "Arrow" perforating tool. Perforate and cut the piece of the fold line which is between the arrows. Emboss the fold line and fold the card. Perforate and cut the six openings and outline. Cut the outer holes of the 4-needle perforations along the outline of the front and back of the card. Open the card, front page faceup, perforate and cut along the lantern and holly and the semicircle perforations.

8 Cut out the lantern using small craft scissors. Emboss the snow on the lantern on the reverse side.

9 Apply some Pergakit glue behind the embossed area of the lantern and fix this three-dimensional element in place. Make a hole in the top of the card (see page 22) and thread through the gold ribbon.

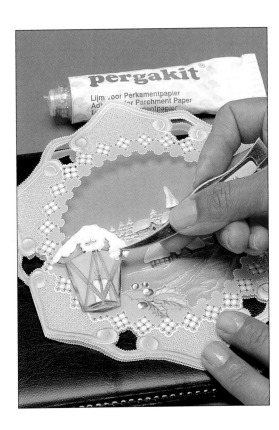

Peacock Wallhanging

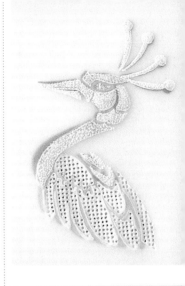

any different wall decorations can be made out of parchment. Vary the central design, the colors and the border according to your own personal preference. This exotic peacock project is built up with layers – parchment, a double mat, a lace border on a green background, a spacer, Rainbow parchment and white paper. The raised border enhances its beauty. Select a frame which will complement the finished project.

You will need

Parchment paper, standard
Template (see page 95)
Adhesive tape, non-permanent
Mapping pen
Tinta ink: white 01T
Large ball embossing tool
"De Luxe" embossing pad
Perga-Soft
1-needle perforating tool
Hard, black cardboard
White pencil
Tinta ink: gold 22T
Paintbrush no.2
Easy-Grid Fine Mesh
"Excellent" perforating pad
"Arrow" perforating tool
4-needle perforating tool
2-needle perforating tool
Pergamano scissors
Extra small ball tool
Rainbow Pastel parchment
Craft knife or scissors
White paper
Double-sided adhesive tape
Cutting mat
Foamcore board ¼" (6 mm) thick
Green paper

1 To create the peacock, trace the template with Tinta white ink onto a sheet of A-4 parchment, positioning the peacock in the center of the sheet. Working on the reverse side, lightly emboss the black areas of the template using the large ball embossing tool. Still on the reverse side, stipple these areas and apply white pencil. Border: use a new A-4 sheet of standard parchment; trace the double-lined scallops with Tinta gold and the square ornaments with Tinta white.

2 On the reverse side paint the grey areas with Tinta white using the brush. Then perforate these areas at the front using the Easy-Grid Fine Mesh and the "Arrow" tool. Border: perforate shallow with the 4-needle tool, following the template.

3 Perforate and cut the openings in the tail using the 2-needle tool and the Pergamano scissors. Border: Emboss on the reverse side with the extra small embossing tool between the double scallops and the lines of the square ornaments.

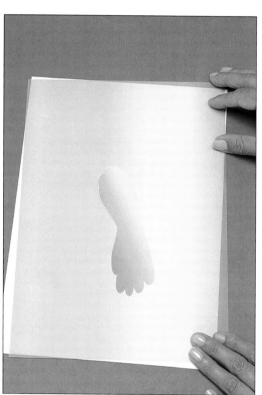

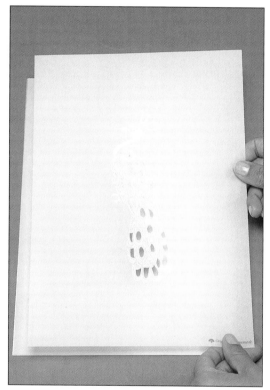

4 In the center of a sheet of Rainbow Pastel parchment trace the shape of the peacock's body and cut out. Take a second piece of Rainbow parchment with a different color pattern, trace the shape of the peacock's body again in the center of the sheet, this time cut it out in such a way to keep the paper intact and create a "window" in the shape of the peacocks body in the center of the paper. Place a sheet of white paper behind the Rainbow pastel parchment with the "window", then place the body shape into the hole. Attach this onto white paper using double-sided tape.

5 Attach the design onto the Rainbow Pastel parchment using double-sided adhesive tape affixed along the outline of the sheet. Border: Perforate deep with the 4-needle tool. Cut the 4-needle perforations into crosses and slits. Perforate with the 2-needle tool along the inner lines of the border, following the template. Cut out these perforations.

6 For the spacer, cut the sheet of foamcore board to the size of your frame and in the center cut out a hole 9" x 4" (23 x 10 cm) in size with a craft knife. Try to cut at a 45° angle.

7 Attach the template onto the green paper. Using a craft knife, cut along the inner scalloped lines of the border. Attach the border onto the green sheet using double-sided adhesive tape and then fix the green paper to the spacer.

8 Make a mat or double mat in matching colors, or buy them with your frame. In this project, a combination of soft green and gold was used.

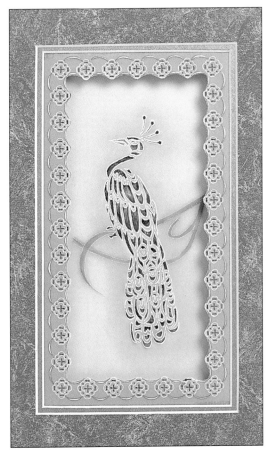

Alternative design

Colored Eyes

This alternative concept is created in a very similar way to the original project – the outlines of the styled feathers are perforated and cut out, the embossing and stippling work is very similar. The difference is that the design is traced a second time, onto another sheet of white parchment. Paint this design using Tinta-Pearl colors, paint the "eyes" in the tail in vivid colors. This sheet is then placed behind the first parchment sheet.

15

PROJECT

Flowers

These parchment flowers look very realistic as much time was spent studying the real thing. Embossing enables the various elements to be shaped in such a way that they approximate the shape of a real flower. Your bunch of parchment flowers will make a beautiful, long-lasting decoration for your home.

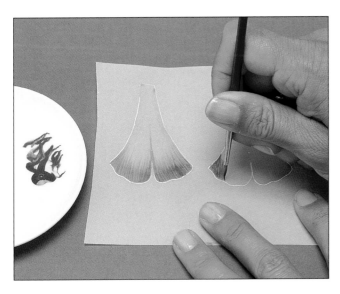

1 On standard parchment trace the five large petals and one bud using Tinta white. Trace the leaves and calyx using Tinta leaf green and paint both sides. Paint the top part of the petals using Pintura bordeaux, painting fine lines, starting from the top of the petals. Paint the remaining parts of the petals using Tinta-Pearl white. Paint the bud in the same way. Cut the petals, bud, calyx and leaves along the outlines with small scissors. Emboss the veining in the leaves using the extra small ball embossing tool.

2 Using the large ball embossing tool emboss the front of all the petals working lengthwise. Then emboss the lines in all the petals on the reverse side, again lengthwise, using the HockeyStick tool.

You will need

Parchment paper, standard

Template (page 94)

Adhesive tape, non-permanent

Mapping pen

Tinta inks: white 01T, leaf green 10T

Pintura paint: bordeaux 51

Tinta-Pearl white 01TP

Paintbrush no.2

Small craft scissors

Extra small ball embossing tool

"De Luxe" embossing pad

Perga-Soft

Large ball embossing tool

HockeyStick embossing tool

Thin green and white florist's wire (26 to 30 gauge)

Paper glue

1 yd. (1 m) heavy green florist's wire (14 to 16 gauge)

Pliers

20 white stamens, medium size

Green florist's tape

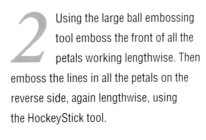

3 To make a leaf, cut off three pieces of thin green florist's wire, partly twist them together, put some glue on them and stick the wire pieces behind the leaves. Do the same for the flower petals, but use white wire.

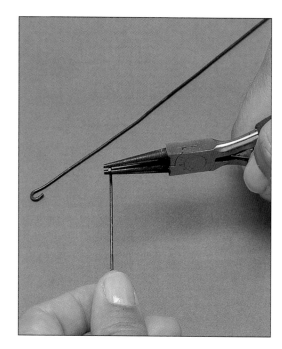

4 For the stamens, bend the end of a length of thick green florist's wire into a "U" shape using a pair of pliers.

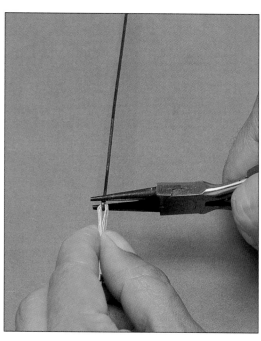

5 Place approximately 10 stamens into the "U" of the wire and close with the pliers.

6 Wind green florist's tape around the stamens and a small part of the stem.

7 Glue two pairs of petals together at the base.

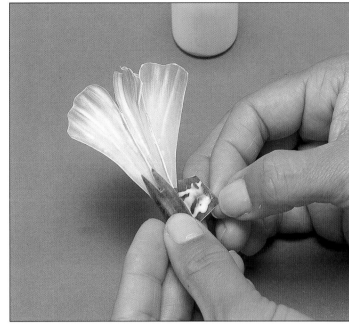

8 Place one pair of petals against the stem and wind the florist's tape around the base of the petals. Then position a second pair of petals, wind tape around it, and finally add one further single petal.

9 Glue the calyx around the base of the petals using paper glue.

10 Keep winding the florist's tape around the stem down to the place where you want to position the first leaf. Place the wire of the leaf against the stem and wind the florist's tape around it. Add the other flowers and leaves in the same way.

Alternative design

Light Lilac

Based on the original project templates you can create flowers of all different sizes and colors. Paint one petal first to judge the result before your prepare the elements for the whole bunch. This alternative bunch have been painted with Tinta-Pearl white and Pintura violet.

Templates

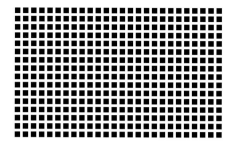

BT5-1 (page 16)

Line
1
2
3
4
5

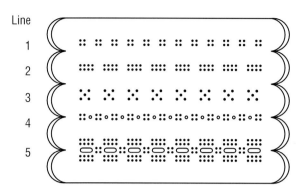

BT4 (page 14)

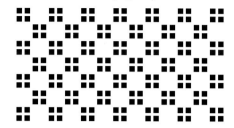

BT5-2 (page 16)

BT2 (page 12)

BT1 (page 11)

BT3 (page 13)

BT9 (page 18)

BT8 (page 18)

BT7 (page 17)

BT6 (page 17)

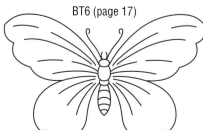

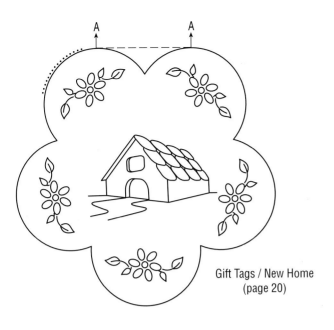

Gift Tags / New Home
(page 20)

Gift Tags / Heart
(page 22)

Gift Tags / Owl
(page 23)

Gift Tags / Flower
(page 23)

Gift Tags / Bear
(page 22)

Gift Envelope
(page 24)

S

S

W

B

Birth Announcement
(page 28)

C

W

A

A

Greeting Card (page 32)

Wedding Card (page 36)

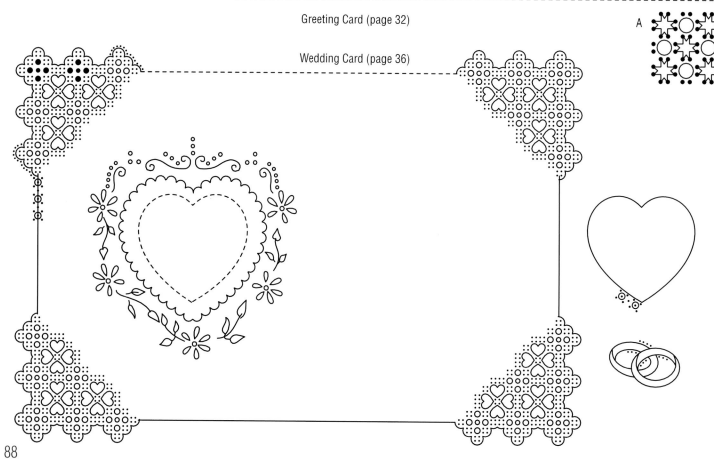

outline insert

Mother's Day Rose Card
(page 50)

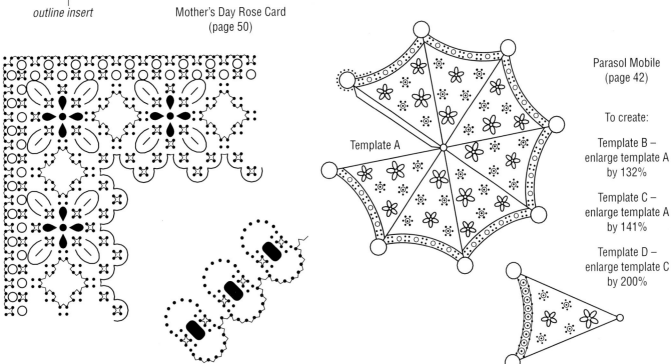

Template A

Parasol Mobile
(page 42)

To create:

Template B –
enlarge template A
by 132%

Template C –
enlarge template A
by 141%

Template D –
enlarge template C
by 200%

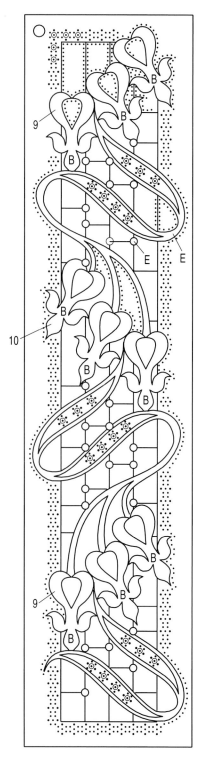

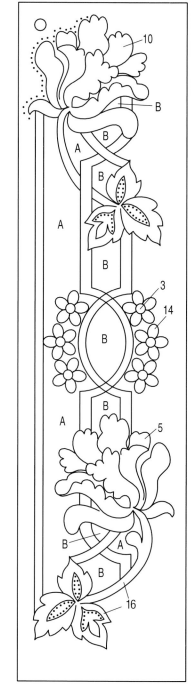

Bookmark (Alternative design)
(page 49)

Bookmark
(page 46)

Fan
(page 54)

 B

 A

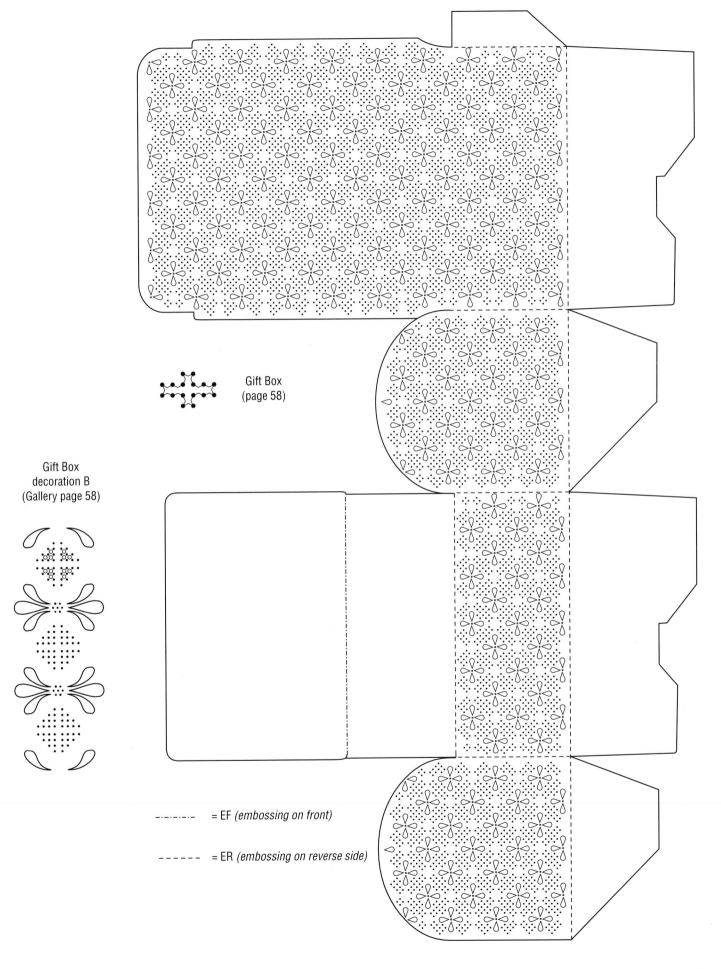

Gift Box
(page 58)

Gift Box
decoration B
(Gallery page 58)

–·–·–·– = EF *(embossing on front)*

– – – – – = ER *(embossing on reverse side)*

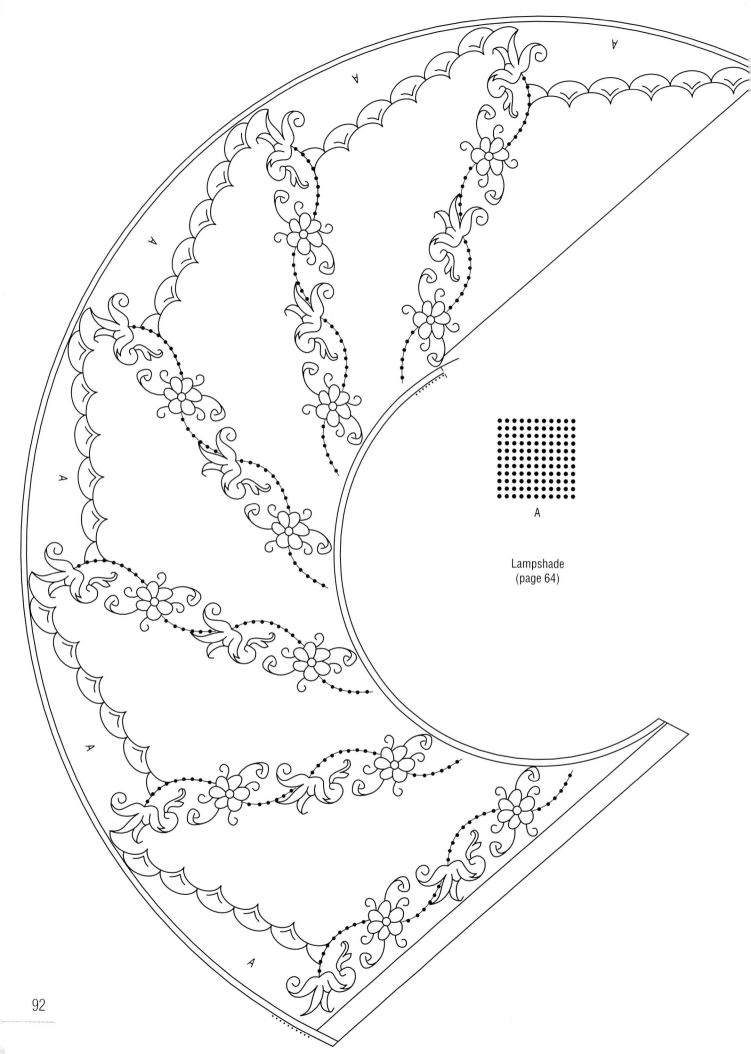

Lampshade
(page 64)

A

Picture Frame
(page 68)

A

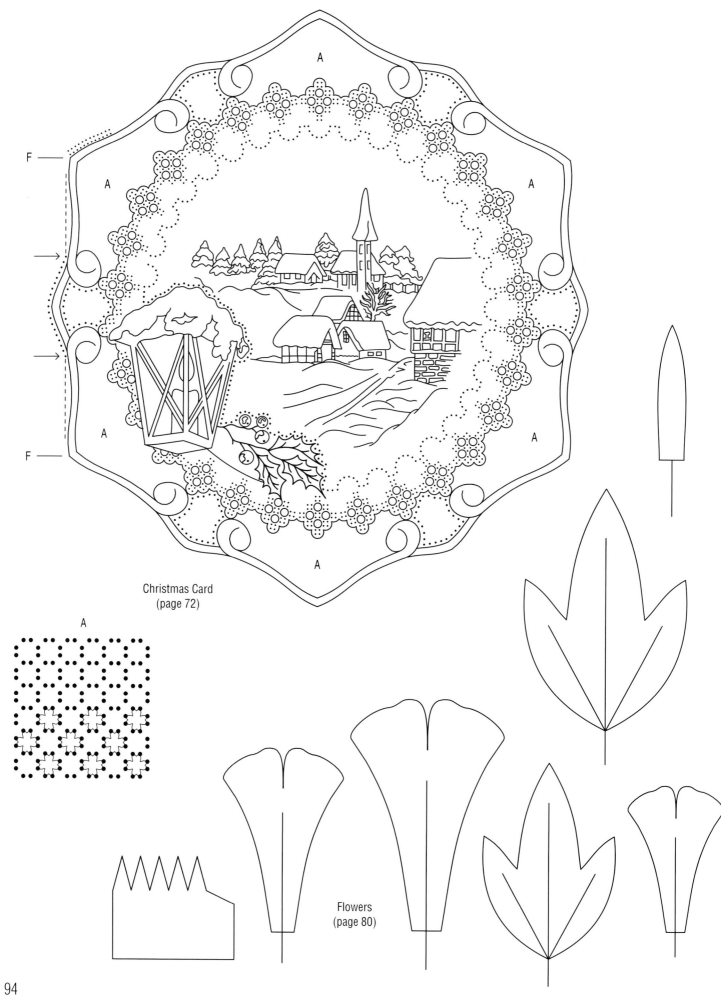

F

A

A

A

A

F

A

A

Christmas Card
(page 72)

A

Flowers
(page 80)

Peacock Wallhanging
(page 76)

Suppliers and Further Information

Pergamano Materials
A catalog with full details of the Pergamano materials for parchment craft plus many project ideas can be obtained from Pergamano suppliers (see below).

Other Pergamano Instruction Books by Martha Ospina
Pergamano: Basic Techniques (tracing, embossing, perforating, cutting, dorsing, stippling) Pergamano: Painting on Parchment

Qualified Pergamano Teachers
Registered Qualified Pergamano Teachers are available in a number of countries. They have been trained by the International Parchment Craft Academy (I.P.C.A.) based in the Netherlands.
Contact the Academy for details:
I.P.C.A. The Netherlands
Info@Pergamano.com

Pergamano Events
In some countries, Pergamano events are held for the public, with demonstrations, exhibitions and workshops. Contact your local office for details.

Pergamano World Magazine
This magazine contains templates with instructions and color photographs of the finished pieces, news about techniques and materials and information on how to use them, further information about events, readers' letters and tips, a pen pal page, etc.

Pergamano International
PO Box 86
1420 AB Uithoorn
The Netherlands
Email: Info@Pergamano.com
www.pergamano.com

PERGAMANO SUPPLIERS

Ecstasy Crafts
R.R. 1
Shanonville, Ontario
KOK 3AO CANADA
E-mail: info@ecstasycrafts.com
www.ecstasycrafts.com

Sweet Impressions
218 1st Ave. S
Kent, WA 98032-5954
(253) 852-6722
www.sweetstamps.com

Best Way Imaging
5419 Seabeck Hwy. NW
Bremerton, WA 98312
(360) 377-0495
www.bestwayimaging.com

Index